GW00578358

Irish Crochet ™

Contents

Annabella Bridal
Necklace

SKILL LEVEL

INTERMEDIATE

FINISHED SIZE
One size fits most

MATERIALS
- Size 20 crochet cotton:
  100 yds white
- Size 5 pearl cotton:
  1 skein white
- Size 10/1.15mm steel crochet hook
- Size F/5/3.75mm crochet hook
  (*padded ring only*)
- Beading needle
- White beads:
  Size 8 or size 10 seed beads: 38
  Size 5mm pearl beads: 11

GAUGE
Gauge is not important for this item.

PATTERN NOTES
Join with slip stitch as indicated unless
  otherwise stated.

When making padding-cord ring, do not wrap
  it too tightly or you will have trouble sliding
  it off the hook and retaining its shape. Leave
  about 1-inch end at beginning and end of wrap.
  This will make it a little easier to handle.

Weave in loose ends as work progresses.

SPECIAL STITCHES
Padded ring: Leaving 1-inch end (*see Pattern
Notes*), wrap size 5 pearl cotton around non-
working end of size F hook number of times
stated in instructions. Leaving 1-inch end,
fasten off. Gently slide lps off hook and insert
hook in ring, yo, pull lp through, yo, pull
through both lps on hook (*sc*).

Beaded single crochet (beaded sc): Insert
hook in st, pull lp through, pull up bead behind
st, yo, pull through all lps on hook.

Beaded double crochet (beaded dc): Yo,
insert hook as indicated in instructions, yo,
pull lp through, yo, pull through 2 lps on hook,
pull up bead behind st, yo, pull through all lps
on hook.

Chain-3 picot (ch-3 picot): Ch 3, sl st in top
of last st worked.

INSTRUCTIONS
NECKLACE
GETTING STARTED
Beads: String seed beads onto crochet cotton.

Padding cord: Cut 2 strands size 5 pearl cotton,
each 15 inches in length, fold in half.

ROSE
Rnd 1: Work **padded ring** (*see Special Stitches*)
with 6 wraps of size 5 pearl cotton, with size 20
crochet cotton, work 12 **beaded sc** (*see Special
Stitches*) in ring, **join** (*see Pattern Notes*) to beg sc.

Rnd 2: Ch 1, sc in first st, ch 3, sk next st, [sc in next st, ch 3, sk next st] around, join in beg sc. *(6 ch sps)*

Rnd 3: Ch 1, (sc, 3 dc, **ch-3 picot**—*see Special Stitches*, 2 dc, sc) in first ch sp and in each ch sp around, join in beg sc. *(6 petals)*

Rnd 4: Working behind petals, **fpsc** *(see Stitch Guide)* around sc on rnd 2, ch 4, [fpsc around next sc on rnd 2, ch 4] around, join in beg fpsc.

Rnd 5: Ch 1, (sc, 4 dc, ch-3 picot, 3 dc, sc) in first ch sp and in each ch sp around, join in beg sc.

Rnd 6: Working behind petals, fpsc around next fpsc on rnd 4, ch 5, [fpsc around next fpsc on rnd 4, ch 5] around, join in beg fpsc.

Rnd 7: Ch 1, (sc, 5 dc, 3-dc picot, 4 dc, sc) in first ch sp and in each ch sp around, join in beg sc. Fasten off.

BORDER

Row 1: With RS facing, join in ch-3 picot on any petal, ch 1, (sc, ch 12, sc) in same picot, ch 6, sc in next picot, ch 8, (sc, ch 12, sc) in next picot, ch 8, sc in next picot, ch 6, (sc, ch 12, sc) in next picot, leaving rem picots unworked, turn.

Row 2: Sl st through center fold of padding cord, ch 1, working over all 4 strands of padding cord unless otherwise stated, work the following steps to complete row:

A. (4 sc, beaded sc, 2 sc, beaded sc, 4 sc) in ch-12 sp, working over padding cord only, 6 sc over cord;

B. (4 sc, beaded sc, 2 sc, beaded sc, 4 sc) in same ch-12 sp, sl st in same picot on petal of Rose;

C. (3 sc, beaded sc, hdc, **beaded dc**—*see Special Stitches*, hdc, beaded sc, 3 sc) in next ch-6 sp, sl st in same worked picot on Rose;

D. (4 sc, beaded sc, hdc, beaded dc, hdc, beaded sc, 4 sc) in next ch-8 sp, sl st in same worked picot on Rose;

E. (4 sc, beaded sc, hdc, beaded dc, hdc, beaded sc, 4 sc, beaded sc, hdc, beaded dc, hdc, beaded sc, 4 sc) in next ch-12 sp, sl st in same picot on Rose;

F. (4 sc, beaded sc, hdc, beaded dc, hdc, beaded sc, 4 sc) in next ch-8 sp, sl st in same worked picot on Rose;

G. (3 sc, beaded sc, hdc, beaded dc, hdc, beaded sc, 3 sc) in next ch-6 sp, sl st in same worked picot on Rose;

H. (4 sc, beaded sc, 2 sc, beaded sc, 4 sc) in next ch-12 sp, working over all 4 strands of padding cord only, 6 sc over cord, (4 sc, beaded sc, 2 sc, beaded sc, 4 sc) in ch-12 sp, sl st in same picot on Rose, leaving rem sts unworked. Fasten off. Trim padding cord close to last st.

FIRST SIDE
GETTING STARTED
Padding-cord: [Cut 2 strands size 5 pearl cotton, each 15 inches in length, fold in half.] twice.

FIRST SIDE
1. Make 11½-inch ch (make longer if larger size is needed);

2. 2 dc in 2nd ch from hook, ch 2, sl st in top of last dc, 2 sc in next ch, sc in next ch;

3. [ch 6, 2 dc in 2nd ch from hook, ch 2, sl st in top of last dc, 2 sc in next ch, sc in next ch] 14 times;

4. ch 4, 3 dc in 2nd ch from hook, sl st in sp created by crocheting over padding cord only on Border, 3 dc in same ch;

5. ch 2, sl st in same ch and through fold of padding cord, work over padding cord unless otherwise stated;

6. 3 dc in each of next 2 chs, [sl st in side of sc of next stem, drop padding cord, ch 4, 2 dc in 2nd ch from hook, ch 2, sl st in same ch, 2 sc in rem chs, sl st in same ch that the sc of corresponding stem was worked into, working over padding cord, sc in next 2 chs] 4 times;

7. sl st in side of sc of next stem, drop padding cord, ch 4, 2 dc in 2nd ch from hook, ch 2, sl st in same ch, 2 sc in each rem ch;

8. sl st into same ch that sc of corresponding stem was worked into, trim padding cord close to last st, sl st in each ch across. Leaving 8-inch end, fasten off.

2ND SIDE
Rep First Side, joining on opposite side of Rose.

ACCENT BEADS
Using long end, sew 5mm bead on end of each tie.

Sew 5mm bead to center of Rose.

Sew 5mm bead to each picot joining on Rose.

Sew 5mm bead on tip closest to the Rose and on each side of piece.

Block. ∎

Irish Crochet
Combs

SKILL LEVEL
INTERMEDIATE

FINISHED SIZE
One size fits most

MATERIALS
- Size 20 crochet cotton:
  100 yds white
  15 yds olive green
- Size 5 pearl cotton:
  1 skein white
- Size 10/1.15mm steel crochet hook
- Size F/5/3.75mm crochet hook
  (padded ring only)
- Beading needle
- Pair hair combs
- White beads:
  Size 8 or size 10 seed beads: 32
  Size 5mm pearl beads: 4
  Size 8mm pearl beads: 2

GAUGE
Gauge is not important for this item.

PATTERN NOTES
Join with slip stitch as indicated unless otherwise stated.

When making padding-cord ring, do not wrap it too tightly or you will have trouble sliding it off the hook and retaining its shape. Leave about 1-inch end at beginning and end of wrap. This will make it a little easier to handle.

Weave in loose ends as work progresses.

SPECIAL STITCHES
Padded ring: **Leaving 1-inch end** (*see Pattern Notes*), wrap crochet cotton around nonworking end of size F hook number of times stated in instructions. Leaving 1-inch end, fasten off. Gently slide lps off hook and insert hook with your working thread in ring, yo, pull lp through, yo, pull through both lps on hook (*sc*).

Cluster (cl): Holding back last lp of each st on hook, 3 dc as indicated in instructions, yo, pull through all lps on hook.

Beaded single crochet (beaded sc): Insert hook in st, pull lp through, pull up bead behind st, yo, pull through all lps on hook.

INSTRUCTIONS
COMB
MAKE 2.
CARNATION
Rnd 1: With green, work **padded ring** (*see Special Stitches*) with 12 wraps, 12 sc in ring, **join** (*see Pattern Notes*) in beg sc. (*12 sc*)

Rnd 2: Working in **front lps** (*see Stitch Guide*), ch 1, sc in first st, *ch 3, **cl** (*see Special Stitches*) in 2nd ch from hook, ch 2, sl st in base of cl, 3 sc over rem ch**, sc in each of next 2 sc, rep from * around, ending last rep at **, sc in last st, join in beg sc. Fasten off.

Rnd 3: Join white in **back lp** (*see Stitch Guide*) of first sc on rnd 1, ch 1, sc in same st, sc in back lp of each st around, join in front lp of beg sc.

Rnd 4: Working in front lps, ch 1, (sc, ch 10, sc) in first st and in each st around, join in beg sc.

Rnd 5: Working in back lps of rnd 3, ch 1, sc in first st, 2 sc in next st, [sc in next st, 2 sc in next st] around, join in beg sc.

Rnd 6: Working in front lps, ch 1, (sc, ch 10, sc) in first st, ch 10, [(sc, ch 10, sc) in next st, ch 10] around, join in beg sc.

Rnd 7: Working in back lps on rnd 5, ch 1, sc in first st, sc in next st, 2 sc in next st, [sc in each of next 2 sts, 2 sc in next st] around, join in beg sc. Leaving 8-inch end, fasten off.

Sew 8mm pearl bead in center of Carnation.

BRIAR ROSE
MAKE 2.
Rnd 1: String 8 beads onto white crochet cotton, work padded ring with 12 wraps, ch 1, [sc in ring, **beaded sc**—*see Special Stitches* in ring] 8 times, join in front lp of beg sc. (*16 sc*)

Rnd 2: Working in front lps, *ch 2, cl in 2nd ch from hook, ch 3**, sc in each of next 2 sc, rep from * around, ending last rep at **, join in back lp of beg sc.

Rnd 3: Working in back lps, ch 1, sc in each st around, join in front lp of beg sc. (*16 sc*)

Rnd 4: Rep rnd 2.

Rnd 5: Rep rnd 3.

Rnd 6: Working in front lps, *ch 2, cl in 2nd ch from hook, ch 3**, sc in each of next 2 sc, rep from * around, ending last rep at **, join in beg sc. Fasten off.

Sew 5mm pearl bead to center of Briar Rose.

LEAF
MAKE 2.

1. Cut 3 strands size 5 pearl cotton, fold in half for padding cord;

2. with white crochet cotton, ch 8, dc in 2nd ch from hook, ch 2, sl st in same ch, 2 sc in next ch, sc in next ch;

3. [ch 7, 2 dc in 2nd ch from hook, ch 2, sl st in same ch, 4 sc over next 2 chs, sc in next ch] twice;

4. [ch 6, 2 dc in 2nd ch from hook, ch 2, sl st in same ch, 2 sc over next ch, sc in next ch] twice;

5. ch 4, 4 dc in 2nd ch from hook, ch 2, sl st in same ch and through fold of padding cord at same time, working over all 6 strands of padding cord unless otherwise stated, 4 sc over next 2 chs;

6. [sl st in side of sc of next stem, drop padding cord, ch 4, 2 dc in 2nd ch from hook, ch 2, sl st in same ch, 2 sc over rem chs, sl st in same ch as sc of corresponding stem was worked, working over padding cord, sc over next 2 chs] twice;

7. [sl st in side of sc on next stem, drop padding cord, ch 5, 2 dc in 2nd ch from hook, ch 2, sl st in same ch, 4 sc over rem chs, sl st in same ch as sc of corresponding stem was worked, working over padding cord, sc over next 2 chs] twice;

8. sl st in side of sc on next stem, drop padding cord, ch 4, 2 dc in 2nd ch from hook, ch 2, sl st in same ch, 2 sc over rem chs, sl st in same ch as sc of corresponding stem, working over padding cord, 4 sc over all but last ch, sc in last ch, trim padding cord close to last sc. Leaving long end, fasten off.

ASSEMBLY
Prepare comb by laying end of crochet cotton across top of comb; secure by wrapping size 5 pearl cotton around top of comb with 6 wraps between each comb tooth. Fasten off. Secure end.

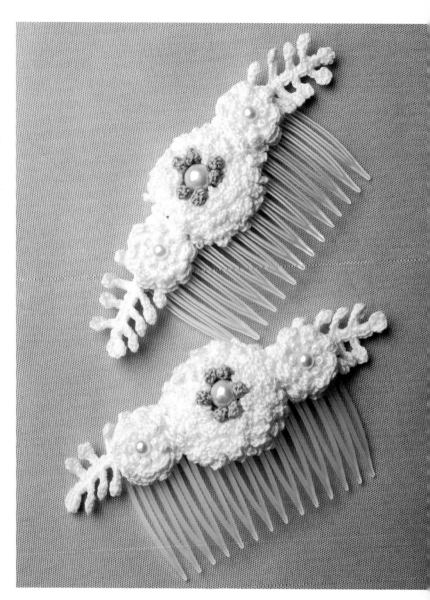

Using 8-inch end, sew Leaves on each end of Comb, leaving 3 branches of the Leaf extended over end of comb.

Using 8-inch end, sew Carnation in center of comb.

Using 8-inch end, sew Briar Roses on each side of Carnation, overlapping leaves.

Rep for 2nd comb. ∎

Ring Bearer
Pillow

SKILL LEVEL

EXPERIENCED

FINISHED SIZE
7½ inches square

MATERIALS
- Size 10 crochet cotton:
  350 yds white
- Size 7/1.65mm steel crochet hook
  or size needed to obtain gauge
- Size H/8/5mm crochet hook
  (padded ring only)
- Sewing needle
- Sewing thread to match fabric
- ¼ yd satin fabric
- Fiberfill
- Embroider floss cards: 2
- 4-inch piece of cardboard
- Stitch marker

GAUGE
11 dc and 10 ch-1 sps = 2 inches; 11 dc rows = 2 inches

PATTERN NOTES
Join with slip stitch as indicated unless otherwise stated.

When making padding-cord ring, do not wrap it too tightly or you will have trouble sliding it off the hook and retaining its shape. Leave about 1-inch end at beginning and end of wrap. This will make it a little easier to handle.

Weave in loose ends as work progresses.

Chain-3 at beginning of row or round counts as first double crochet and chain-1 unless otherwise stated.

SPECIAL STITCHES
Padded ring: Leaving 1-inch end (*see Pattern Notes*), wrap crochet cotton around non-working end of size H hook number of times stated in instructions, leaving 1-inch end, fasten off. Gently slide lps off hook and insert hook in ring, yo, pull lp through, yo, pull through both lps on hook (*sc*).

Triple picot: Ch 4, sl st in front lp and front strand of last st worked, ch 5, sl st in same st catching front lp of first ch of beg ch-4, ch 4, sl st in same st catching front lp of beg ch-4 and ch-5.

Chain-3 picot (ch-3 picot): Ch 3, sl st in top of last st worked.

INSTRUCTIONS
GETTING STARTED
First cord: Cut 3 strands, each 15 inches in length, fold in half.

2nd cord: Cut 3 strands, each 8 feet in length, fold in half.

Use floss card to wind padding cord on so you have only small length to deal with at a time. Wind strands onto card beg with end farthest away from fold so the fold will be on outside when wound.

FRONT

Rnd 1: With first padding cord, make **padded ring** (see Special Stitches) with 15 wraps, 16 sc in ring, **join** (see Pattern Notes) in beg sc. (16 sc)

Rnd 2: Ch 6, sk next sc, [dc in next sc, ch 3, sk next sc] around, join in 3rd ch of beg ch-6.

Rnd 3: Sl st through fold of first padding cord, sc in same st, working over all 6 strands of first cord around, 5 sc in next ch-3 sp, [sc in next dc, 5 sc in next ch-3 sp] around, join in beg sc. (48 sc)

Rnd 4: Ch 1, continue to work over padding cord, sc in each st around, join in **front lp** (see Stitch Guide) of beg sc. Fasten off padding cord.

Rnd 5: Ch 1, sc in first st, mark **back lp** (see Stitch Guide) of first st on rnd 4, working in front lps, ch 5, sc in same st, ch 5, [(sc, ch 5, sc) in next st, ch 5] around, join in beg sc.

Rnd 6: Ch 1, sl st in marked back lp, ch 1, sc in each st around, join in front lp of beg sc.

Rnd 7: Ch 1, sc in first st, mark back lp of first st on rnd 6, working in front lps, ch 6, sc in same st, [(sc, ch 6, sc) in next st, ch 6] around, join in beg sc. Mark every 6th st from first marked st in back lp on rnd 6.

Rnd 8: Ch 1, sl st in marked st, working in back lps, ch 2, dc in same st, mark last st, 2 dc in each st around, move markers to 2nd dc of each dc group, join in 2nd ch of beg ch-2. (96 dc)

FIRST PETAL

Row 1: Now working in rows, sl st in marked dc, ch 4, sk next 2 dc, dc in next dc, [ch 2, sk next 2 dc, dc in next dc] twice, leaving rem dc unworked, turn.

Row 2: Sl st in first ch sp, ch 4, dc in same ch sp, [ch 2, dc in next ch-2 sp] twice, ch 2, dc in same ch sp, turn.

Row 3: Sl st in first ch sp, ch 4, dc in same ch sp, [ch 2, dc in next ch-2 sp] across, ch 2, dc in same ch sp, turn.

Row 4: Ch 4, dc in same ch sp, [ch 2, dc in next ch-2 sp] 4 times, dc in same ch sp. Fasten off.

2ND–8TH PETALS

Row 1: Join in next marked dc, ch 4, sk next 2 sts, dc in next st, [ch 2, sk next 2 sts, dc in next st] twice, leaving rem sts unworked, turn.

Rows 2–4: Rep rows 2–4 of First Petal.

EDGING

First Petal: With 2nd padding cord, join with sc in sc next to Petal that will have you working toward Petal, be sure to adjust the padding cord at the end of each straight section by gently tugging on all strands at once, working over padding cord unless otherwise stated. Work the following steps to complete rnd:

A. 4 sc in end of each of next 3 rows, (2 sc, **ch-3 picot**—*see Special Stitches*, {2 sc, ch-3 picot} twice, 2 sc) in next corner sp on Petal;

B. (2 sc, ch-3 picot, 2 sc) in next ch-2 sp, 4 sc in next ch-2 sp, sc in next dc, 3 sc in next ch-2 sp, drop padding cord, ch 2, **turn**;

C. (dc, ch 2, dc) in sc above dc, ch 2, sk next 2 sc, sc in next sc, sl st in next sc, ch 1, **turn**;

D. (2 sc, ch-3 picot, sc) in each of next 3 ch-2 sps, pick padding cord back up, sc in same ch-2 sp *(Petal)*, (2 sc, ch-3 picot, 2 sc) in next ch-2 sp, (2 sc, ch-3 picot, {2 sc, ch-3 picot} twice, 2 sc) in next corner sp, 4 sc in each of next 3 rows on side of Petal, sc in each of next 2 sc;

2nd–7th Petals:

A. 4 sc in each of next 3 rows on side of Petal, 2 sc in next corner sp on Petal, ch 1, sl st in first picot in corner sp on previous Petal;

B. ch 1, sl st in last sc, (2 sc, {ch-3 picot, 2 sc} twice) in same corner sp on this Petal, (2 sc, ch-3 picot, 2 sc) in next ch-2 sp;

C. 4 sc in next ch-2 sp, sc in next dc, 3 sc in next ch-2 sp, drop padding cord, ch 2, turn;

D. (dc, ch 2, dc) in sc above dc, ch 2, sk next 2 sc, sc in next sc, sl st in next sc, ch 1, turn;

E. (2 sc, ch-3 picot, sc) in each of next 3 ch-2 sps, pick padding cord back up, sc in same ch sp *(Petal)*, (2 sc, ch-3 picot, {2 sc, ch-3 picot} twice, 2 sc) in next corner ch sp, 4 sc in each of next 3 rows on side of Petal, sc in each of next 2 sc;

8th Petal:

A. 4 sc in each of next 3 rows on side of Petal, 2 sc in next corner sp on Petal, ch 1, sl st in first picot in corner sp on previous Petal, ch 1, sl st in last sc;

B. (2 sc, {ch-3 picot, 2 sc} twice) in same corner sp on this Petal, (2 sc, ch-3 picot, 2 sc) in next ch-2 sp, 4 sc in next ch-2 sp, sc in next dc, 3 sc in next ch-2 sp, drop padding cord, ch 2, turn;

C. (dc, ch 2, dc) in sc above dc, ch 2, sk next 2 sc, sc in next sc, sl st in next sc, ch 1, turn;

D. (2 sc, ch-3 picot, sc) in each of next 3 ch-2 sps, pick padding cord back up, sc in same ch sp, (2 sc, ch-3 picot, 2 sc) in next ch-2 sp, (2 sc, {ch-3 picot, 2 sc} twice) in next corner ch sp;

E. ch 1, sl st in picot closest to center of First Petal, ch 1, sl st in last sc on this Petal, 2 sc in same ch sp, 4 sc in each of next 3 rows on side of Petal, sc in last sc, join in beg sc. Fasten off.

CORNER PICOT POINTS
Wrap 55 feet of crochet cotton onto floss card.

1. Work padded ring with 15 wraps, 3 sc in ring, ch-3 picot, 2 sc in ring, ch 2;

2. work padded ring with 15 wraps, [4 sc in this ring, ch-3 picot] 3 times, 4 sc in same ring, 3 sc around ch-2, 2 sc in first ring, ch 3;

3. work padded ring with 15 wraps, 3 sc in this ring, ch 1, sl st in last picot on previous ring, ch 1, sl st in last sc on this ring, 5 sc in same ring, **triple picot** (*see Special Stitches*), 5 sc in same ring, ch-3 picot, 3 sc in same ring, 4 sc around ch-3, 2 sc in first ring, ch 2;

4. work padded ring with 15 wraps, 4 sc in this ring, ch 1, sl st in last picot on previous ring, [4 sc in same ring, ch-3 picot] twice, 4 sc in same ring, 3 sc around ch-2, (2 sc, ch-3 picot, 3 sc) in first ring, ch 1, sl st in center picot on arch of any Petal, ch 1, sl st in last sc, join in beg sc. Fasten off.

5. Rep Corner Picot Point 3 times, sk 1 Petal between corners.

SIDE PICOT RINGS
Work padded ring with 15 wraps, [4 sc in ring, ch-3 picot] 3 times, 4 sc in same ring, ch 1, sl st in center picot on arch of any free Petal, ch 1, sl st in last sc, join in beg sc. Fasten off.

Rep on each rem free Petal.

CONNECTING RING A
Work padded ring with 15 wraps, 4 sc in ring, ch-3 picot, 4 sc in same ring, ch 1, sl st in outside picot on Corner Picot Point, ch 1, sl st in last sc, [4 sc in ring, ch-3 picot] twice, join in beg sc. Fasten off.

Rep around 7 times.

CONNECTING RING B
Work padded ring with 15 wraps, 4 sc in ring, ch-3 picot, 4 sc in ring, ch 1, sk next picot on Connecting Ring A, sl st in next picot, ch 1, sl st in last sc, 4 sc in ring, ch-3 picot, 4 sc in ring, ch 1, sl st in side picot on Side Picot Ring on Petal, ch 1, sl st in last sc, join in beg sc. Fasten off.

Rep around 7 times.

FILL-IN RING A
Work padded ring with 15 wraps, 2 sc in ring, ch-3 picot, 2 sc in ring, ch 1, sl st in inside picot of Connecting Ring A on any corner, ch 1, sl st in last sc, 2 sc in ring, ch-3 picot, 2 sc in ring, ch 1, sk 2 picot on Petal counting from Corner Picot Point, sl st in next picot, ch 1, sl st in last sc, 2 sc in same ring, ch-3 picot, 2 sc in ring, ch 1, sk next picot on next Petal, ch 1, sl st in next picot on Petal, ch 1, sl st in last sc, 2 sc in ring, ch-3 picot, 2 sc in ring, ch 1, sl st in picot on Connecting Ring B, ch 1, sl st in last sc, join in beg sc. Fasten off.

Rep around 3 times in corresponding corners.

FILL-IN RING B
Work padded ring with 15 wraps, 2 sc in ring, ch-3 picot, 2 sc in ring, ch 1, sl st in inside picot on Connecting Ring B on any corner, ch 1, sl st in last sc, 2 sc in ring, ch-3 picot, 2 sc in ring, ch 1, sk next 2 picot on Petal counting from Side Picot Ring connection, sl st in next picot, ch 1, sl st in last sc, 2 sc in ring, ch-3 picot, 2 sc in ring, ch-3 picot, 2 sc in ring, ch 1, sk next picot on next Petal, sl st in next picot, ch 1, sl st in last sc, 2 sc in ring, ch-3 picot, 2 sc in ring, ch 1, sl st in picot on Connecting Ring A, ch 1, sl st in last sc, join in beg sc. Fasten off.

Rep around 3 times on corresponding corners.

EDGING
Rnd 1: With RS facing, join in free picot on any of Side Picot Ring, ch 1, sc in same picot, *ch 5, sc in next picot, ch 7, hdc in next picot, ch 5, dc in next picot, ch 9, (tr, ch 6, tr) in center lp of triple picot at corner, ch 9, dc in next picot, ch 5, hdc in next picot, ch 7, sc in next picot, ch 5**, sc in next picot, rep from * around, ending last rep at **, join in beg sc.

Rnd 2: Sl st in first ch-5 sp, ch 1, 6 sc in same ch sp, *8 sc in next ch-7 sp, 6 sc in next ch-5 sp, 10 sc in next ch-9 sp, 8 sc in next ch-6 sp, 10 sc in next ch-9 sp, 6 sc in next ch-5 sp, 8 sc in next ch-7 sp, 6 sc in next ch-5 sp**, 6 sc in next ch-5 sp, rep from * around, ending last rep at **, join in beg sc.

Rnd 3: Ch 3 (*see Pattern Notes*), sk next sc, dc in next sc, [ch 1, sk next sc, dc in next sc] 15 times, *ch 1, (dc, ch 1, dc) in next sc, ch 1, dc in next sc, [ch 1, sk next sc, dc in next sc] 33 times, rep from * 3 times, ch 1, (dc, ch 1, dc) in next sc, ch 1, dc in next sc, [ch 1, sk next st, dc in next sc] across, ch 1, sk last st, join in 3rd ch of beg ch-3.

Rnd 4: Sl st in first ch sp, ch 1, 2 sc in same ch sp, 2 sc in each of next 16 ch-1 sps, 3 sc in next ch-1 sp, [2 sc in each of next 35 ch-1 sps, 3 sc in next ch-1 sp] 3 times, 2 sc in each of last 18 ch-1 sps, join in beg sc. Fasten off. (29 sc)

BACK

Row 1: Ch 77, dc in 5th ch from hook, [ch 1, sk next ch, dc in next ch] across, turn. (38 dc)

Rows 2–37: Ch 3, sk all ch sps, dc in next dc, [ch 1, dc in next dc] across, turn.

EDGING

Ch 1, 2 sc in first ch sp, *2 sc in each of next 35 ch-1 sps, 3 sc in next corner ch sp, working in ends of rows, 2 sc in end of each of next 35 rows*, 3 sc in corner, rep between * once, sc in same corner as beg sc. Fasten off. (292 sc)

PILLOW

Cut 2 pieces of fabric, each 8½ inches square.

With RS tog, sew pieces tog, allowing ¼ inch for seam around, leaving last 3 inches open.

Turn RS out and stuff with fiberfill.

Sew opening closed.

EDGING

Holding Front and Back WS tog, working around outer edge through both thicknesses, join in back lp of first sc in corner, ch 1, sc in same st, *2 sc in next sc (this should be the center sc on corner), ch 4, sl st in last sc, sc in same sc, sc in each of next 2 sc, ch-3 picot, [sc in each of next 4 sts, ch-3 picot] 17 times, sc in each of next 2 sc, rep from * twice, insert Pillow when 3 sides have been completed, 2 sc in next sc (this should be center sc on corner), ch 4, sl st in last sc, sc in same sc, sc in each of next 2 sc, ch-3 picot, [sc in each of next 4 sc, ch-3 picot] 17 times, sc in each of next 2 sts, join in beg sc. Fasten off.

TASSEL
MAKE 4.

Wrap crochet cotton around 4-inch piece of cardboard 25 times, cut crochet cotton, using crochet hook, pull strand of cotton under wrapped cotton at top of cardboard. Leaving 5-inch end at beg and end, cut cotton and tie as tight as you can.

Cut wrapped crochet cotton at bottom edge of cardboard. Set aside.

Leaving 5-inch end, ch 12, sl st in first ch to form ring. Leaving 5-inch end, fasten off.

Insert Tassel into ring, match center knot and ring joining tog, fold Tassel in half, covering both knot and joining.

Wrap separate strand around all strands 12 to 15 times, below fold.

Comb out Tassels and trim edges. Be sure to trim all your Tassels the same length.

Attach Tassel to Pillow by inserting ch lp on Tassel through ch-4 lps on the corner of the Pillow, pull Tassel through the ch lp on Tassel again to secure.

Be sure to pull through the same way on each corner so they match. ■

Irish Isle
Doily

SKILL LEVEL

INTERMEDIATE

FINISHED SIZE
20 inches across

MATERIALS
- Size 10 crochet cotton:
  - 200 yds pink
  - 150 yds white
  - 125 yds green
- Size 7/1.65mm steel crochet hook or size needed to obtain gauge
- Size G/6/4mm crochet hook *(padded ring only)*
- Stitch marker

GAUGE
Rose = 1¾ inches across

PATTERN NOTES
This doily is constructed a little differently than normal: Begin by making a ring of 6 Motifs with a large open space in center. The Center Motif is worked next and the Fill-In Roses are worked last.

Join with slip stitch as indicated unless otherwise stated.

When making padding-cord ring, do not wrap it too tightly or you will have trouble sliding it off the hook and retaining its shape. Leave about 1-inch end at beginning and end of wrap. This will make it a little easier to handle.

Weave in loose ends as work progresses.

SPECIAL STITCHES
Padded ring: Leaving 1-inch end *(see Pattern Notes)*, wrap crochet cotton around non-working end of size G hook number of times stated in instructions. Leaving 1-inch end, fasten off. Gently slide lps off hook and insert hook in ring, yo, pull lp through, yo, pull through both lps on hook *(sc)*.

Triple picot: Ch 4, sl st in **front lp** *(see Stitch Guide)* and front strand of last st worked, ch 5, sl st in same st, catching front lp of first ch of beg ch-4, ch 4, sl st in same st, catching front lp of beg ch-4 and ch-5.

Chain-3 picot (ch-3 picot): Ch 3, sl st in top of last st worked.

2-treble cluster (2-tr cl): Holding back last lp of each st on hook, 2 tr as indicated in instructions, yo, pull through all lps on hook.

INSTRUCTIONS
DOILY
FIRST ROSE MOTIF
Rnd 1: With pink, work **padded ring** (*see Special Stitches*) with 10 wraps, 16 sc in ring, **join** (*see Pattern Notes*) in beg sc. (*16 sc*)

Rnd 2: Ch 1, sc in first st, ch 3, sk next st, [sc in next st, ch 3, sk next st] around, join in beg sc. (*8 ch sps*)

Rnd 3: Ch 1, (sc, 5 dc, sc) in first ch sp and in each ch sp around, join in beg sc. (*8 petals*)

Rnd 4: Ch 1, working behind petals, **fpsc** (*see Stitch Guide*) around first sc on rnd 2, ch 4, [fpsc around next sc on rnd 2, ch 4] around, join in beg fpsc.

Rnd 5: Ch 1, (sc, 7 dc, sc) in first ch sp and in each ch sp around, join in beg sc.

Rnd 6: Ch 1, working behind petals, fpsc around first sc on rnd 4 of next petal, ch 5, [fpsc around next sc on rnd 4, ch 5] around, join in beg fpsc.

Rnd 7: Ch 1, (sc, 9 dc, sc) in first ch sp and in each ch sp around, join in beg sc. Fasten off.

FIRST LEAF
Row 1: With green, ch 9, sc in 2nd ch from hook and in each ch across, ch 3, working on opposite side of ch, sc in each of next 6 chs, leaving rem chs unworked, turn.

Row 2: Working in **back lps** (*see Stitch Guide*), ch 2, sc in 2nd ch from hook, sc in each of first 6 sc, (sc, ch 3, sc) in ch-3 sp, sc in each of next 6 sc, leaving rem sts unworked, turn.

Row 3: Ch 2, sc in 2nd ch from hook, working in back lps, sc in each of next 7 sc, (sc, ch 3, sc) in next ch-3 sp, sc in each of next 6 sc, leaving rem sts unworked, turn.

Next rows: Rep row 3 until you have 1 center point and 4 side points on 1 side and up to 4th point on final side, turn.

Last row: Ch 2, sc in 2nd ch from hook, working in back lps, sc in each of first 7 sc, sc in next ch-3 sp, sl st in sp between 2 petals on Rose, sc in same ch sp, sl st in next sc on side of Leaf, leaving rem sts unworked. Fasten off.

2ND–4TH LEAVES
Work same as First Leaf up to last row.

Last row: Ch 2, sc in 2nd ch from hook, working in back lps, sc in each of first 7 sc, sc in next ch-3 sp, sk next petal on Rose, sl st in sp between next 2 petals on Rose, sc in same ch sp, sl st in next sc on side of Leaf, leaving rem sts unworked. Fasten off.

EDGING
Rnd 1: Join white in sp between petals on Rose and between Leaves, ch 7, *sl st in first tip of Leaf, [ch 4, sl st in next tip on Leaf] 3 times, ch 5, sl st in tip of Leaf at top, ch 5, sl st in next tip of Leaf, [ch 4, sl st in next tip on Leaf] 3 times, ch 4**, tr in next sp between petals on Rose between Leaves, rep from * around, ending last rep at **, join in 3rd ch of beg ch-7.

Rnd 2: Sl st in first ch sp, ch 1, *(3 sc, **ch-3 picot**—*see Special Stitches*, 2 sc) in same ch sp, (sc, 2 dc, ch-3 picot, dc, sc) in each of next 3 ch sps, (sc, 5 dc) in next ch-5 sp, dc in next sc, **triple picot** (*see Stitch Guide*) in last dc worked, dc in same sc, (5 dc, sc) in next ch-5 sp, (sc, 2 dc, ch-3 picot, dc, sc) in each of next 3 ch-4 sps, (3 sc, ch 3-picot, 2 sc) in next ch sp, rep from * around, join in beg sc. Fasten off.

FIRST STAR FLOWER
With pink, ch 4, **2-tr cl** (*see Special Stitches*) in 4th ch from hook, ch-3 picot, ch 3, sl st in 4th ch, [ch 3, 2-tr cl in same ch, ch-3 picot, ch 3, sl st in same ch] twice, ch 3, 2-tr cl in same ch, ch 1, sl st in 2nd picot from tr on rnd 1 of Edging that is between Leaves that will have you working toward tr, ch 1, sl st in top of cl, ch 3, sl st in same ch, ch 3, 2-tr cl in same ch, ch 1, sk next 2 picot, sl st in next picot, ch 1, sl st in top of cl, ch 3, sl st in same st as last petal. Fasten off.

2ND–4TH STAR FLOWERS
Rep First Star Flower 3 times between Leaves.

STAR FLOWER ARCH
Row 1: With WS facing, join white in picot on Edging before Star Flower at any Leaf point that will have you working toward the Star Flower, [ch 5, sc in next ch sp on Star Flower] 3 times, ch 5, (sc, sl st) in next free picot on Edging at next Leaf point, leaving rem sts unworked, turn.

Row 2: Ch 1, (sc, 3 dc, ch-3 picot, 2 dc, sc) in next ch-5 sp, (sc, 7 dc) in next ch-5 sp, (dc, triple picot, dc) in next sc, (7 dc, sc) in next ch-5 sp, (sc, 3 dc, ch-3 picot, 2 dc, sc) in last ch-5 sp, sl st in same worked picot on Edging. Fasten off.

Rep over rem Star Flowers.

2ND ROSE MOTIF
Rnds 1–7: Rep rnds 1–7 of First Rose Motif.

LEAVES
Work same as Leaves on First Rose Motif.

EDGING
Rnd 1: Rep rnd 1 of Edging on First Rose Motif.

Rnd 2: Sl st in first ch sp, ch 1, (3 sc, ch-3 picot, 2 sc) in same ch sp, work the following steps to complete rnd:

  A. *(Sc, 2 dc, ch-3 picot, dc, sc) in each of next 3 ch sps, (sc, 5 dc) in next ch-5 sp, dc in next sc, triple picot in last dc worked, dc in same sc;

  B. (5 dc, sc) in next ch-5 sp, (sc, 2 dc, ch-3 picot, dc, sc) in each of next 3 ch-4 sps, (3 sc, ch-3 picot, 2 sc) in each of next 2 ch-4 sps, rep from * in step A 3 times;

  C. (sc, 2 dc, ch-3 picot, dc, sc) in each of next 3 ch-4 sps, (sc, 5 dc) in next ch-5 sp, dc in next sc, ch 4, sl st in last dc;

  D. ch 2, sl st in ch-5 sp on any triple picot on Edging at Leaf point of last Rose Motif, ch 2, sl st in same dc, catching front lp of first ch-4 where you sl st in top of dc;

  E. ch 4, sl st in same st, catching front lps of ch-4 and last ch-2, dc in same st, (5 dc, sc) in next ch-5 sp, (sc, 2 dc, ch-3 picot, dc, sc) in each of next 3 ch-5 sps, (3 sc, ch-3 picot, 2 sc) in last ch-4 sp, join in beg sc. Fasten off.

STAR FLOWERS
Work same as Star Flowers on First Rose Motif.

STAR FLOWER ARCH
Row 1: Rep row 1 of Star Flower Arch of First Rose Motif.

Row 2: Ch 1, (sc, 3 dc, ch-3 picot, 2 dc, sc) in next ch-5 sp, (sc, 7 dc) in next ch-5 sp, dc in next sc, ch 4, sl st in top of last dc, ch 2, sl st in ch-5 sp on corresponding triple picot on last Rose Motif, ch 2, sl st in same dc, catching front lp of first ch-4 lp, ch 4, sl st in same dc, catching front lp of ch-4 and ch-2, dc in same sc as last dc, (7 dc, sc) in next ch-5 sp, (sc, 3 dc, ch-3 picot, 2 dc, sc) in last ch-5 sp, sl st in same worked picot. Fasten off.

Rep Star Flower Arch of First Rose Motif over rem Star Flowers.

3RD–5TH ROSE MOTIFS
Work same as 2nd Rose Motif.

6TH ROSE MOTIF
Work same as 2nd Rose Motif up to Edging.

EDGING
Rnd 1: Rep rnd 1 of Edging on First Rose Motif.

Rnd 2: Sl st in first ch sp, ch 1, (3 sc, ch-3 picot, 2 sc) in same ch sp, work the following steps to complete rnd:

  A. *(Sc, 2 dc, ch-3 picot, dc, sc) in each of next 3 ch sps, (sc, 5 dc) in next ch-5 sp, dc in next sc, triple picot in last dc worked, dc in same sc;

  B. (5 dc, sc) in next ch-5 sp, (sc, 2 dc, ch-3 picot, dc, sc) in each of next 3 ch-4 sps, (3 sc, ch-3 picot, 2 sc) in each of next 2 ch-4 sps, rep from * in step A once;

  C. **(sc, 2 dc, ch-3 picot, dc, sc) in each of next 3 ch sps, (sc, 5 dc) in next ch-5 sp, dc in next sc, ch 4, sl st in last dc;

D. ch 2, sl st in ch-5 sp on any triple picot on Edging at Leaf point of corresponding Rose Motif, ch 2, sl st in same dc, catching front lp of first ch-4 where you sl st in top of dc;

E. ch 4, sl st in same st, catching front lps of ch-4 and last ch-2, dc in same st, (5 dc, sc) in next ch-5 sp, (sc, 2 dc, ch-3 picot, dc, sc) in each of next 3 ch-5 sps**;

F. (3 sc, ch-3 picot, 2 sc) in each of next 2 ch-4 sps, rep between ** in steps C and E once, (3 sc, ch-3 picot, 2 sc) in last ch sp, join in beg sc. Fasten off.

STAR FLOWERS
Work same as Star Flowers on First Rose Motif.

STAR FLOWER ARCHS
Work Star Flower Arch of 2nd Rose Motif over Star Flowers next to Leaves that are joined to Rose Motifs.

CENTER ROSE MOTIF
Rnd 1: With pink, work padded ring with 10 wraps, 12 sc in ring, join in beg sc. *(12 sc)*

Rnd 2: Ch 1, sc in first st, ch 3, sk next st, [sc in next st, ch 3, sk next st] around, join in beg sc. *(6 ch sps)*

Rnd 3: Ch 1, (sc, 5 dc, sc) in first ch sp and in each ch sp around, join in beg sc. *(6 petals)*

Rnd 4: Ch 1, working behind petals, fpsc around first sc on rnd 2, ch 4, [fpsc around next sc on rnd 2, ch 4] around, join in beg fpsc.

Rnd 5: Ch 1, (sc, 7 dc, sc) in first ch sp and in each ch sp around, join in beg sc.

Rnd 6: Ch 1, working behind petals, fpsc around first sc on rnd 4, ch 5, [fpsc around next sc on rnd 4, ch 5] around, join in beg fpsc.

Rnd 7: Ch 1, (sc, 9 dc, sc) in first ch sp and in each ch sp around, join in beg sc. Fasten off.

FIRST LEAF
Row 1: With green, ch 9, sc in 2nd ch from hook and in each ch across, ch 3, working on opposite side of ch, sc in each of next 6 chs, leaving rem chs unworked, turn.

Row 2: Ch 2, sc in 2nd ch from hook, working in back lps, sc in each of first 6 sc, (sc, ch 3, sc) in next ch-3 sp, working in back lps, sc in each of next 6 sc, leaving rem sts unworked, turn.

Row 3: Ch 2, sc in 2nd ch from hook, working in back lps, sc in each of first 7 sc, (sc, ch 3, sc) in next ch-3 sp, working in back lps, sc in each of next 6 sc, leaving rem sts unworked, turn.

Next rows: Rep row 3 until you have 1 center point and 3 side points on 1 side and up to 3rd point on final side.

Last row: Ch 2, sc in 2nd ch from hook, working in back lps, sc in each of first 7 sts, (sc, sl st between 2 petals on Rose, sc) in ch-3 sp, sl st in next sc on side of Leaf, leaving rem sts unworked. Fasten off.

2ND–5TH LEAVES
Work same as First Leaf up to Last row.

Last row: Ch 1, sl st in 3rd Leaf point on previous Leaf, ch 1, sc in 2nd ch from hook, working in back lps, sc in each of first 7 sc, (sc, sl st between next 2 petals on Rose, sc) in ch-3 sp, sl st in next sc, leaving rem sts unworked. Fasten off.

LAST LEAF
Rows 1–3: Rep rows 1–3 of First Leaf.

Next rows: Rep row 3 until you have 1 center point and 2 side points on 1 side and up to 3rd point on final side.

Next row: Ch 1, sl st in 3rd Leaf point on previous Leaf, ch 1, sc in 2nd ch from hook, working in back lps, sc in each of first 7 sc, (sc, ch 3, sc) in next ch-3 sp, working in back lps, sc in each of next 6 sc, leaving rem sc unworked, turn.

Last row: Ch 1, sl st in 3rd Leaf point on previous Leaf, ch 1, sc in 2nd ch from hook, working in back lps, sc in each of first 7 sc, (sc, sl st between next 2 petals on Rose, sc) in ch-3 sp, sl st in next sc, leaving rem sts unworked. Fasten off.

EDGING

Rnd 1: Join white in any joining between Leaves, ch 4 *(counts as first dc and ch-2)*, *sc in next Leaf point, ch 4, sc in next Leaf point, ch 5, sc in tip of Leaf, ch 5, sc in next Leaf point, ch 4, sc in next Leaf point, ch 2**, dc in next joining between Leaves, ch 2, rep from * around, ending last rep at **, join in 2nd ch of beg ch-4.

Rnd 2: Ch 1, sc in first st, ch-3 picot, *2 sc in next ch-2 sp, (sc, 2 dc, ch-3 picot, dc, sc) in next ch-4 sp, (sc, 5 dc) in next ch-5 sp, dc in next sc, ch 4, sl st in last dc, ch 2, sl st in ch-5 lp on triple picot on any Star Flower Arch, ch 2, sl st in same dc, catching front lp of ch-4, ch 4, sl st in same dc, catching front lp of first ch 4 and last ch-2, dc in same sc as last dc, (5 dc, sc) in next ch-5 sp, (sc, 2 dc, ch-3 picot, dc, sc) in next ch-4 sp, 2 sc in next ch-2 sp**, sc in next dc, ch-3 picot, rep from * around, ending last rep at **, join in beg sc. Fasten off.

FIRST FILL-IN ROSE

Rnd 1: With pink, work padded ring with 10 wraps, 16 sc in ring, join in beg sc. *(16 sc)*

Rnd 2: Ch 1, sc in first st, ch 3, sk next st, [sc in next st, ch 3, sk next st] around, join in beg sc. *(8 ch sps)*

Rnd 3: Ch 1, (sc, 5 dc, sc) in first ch sp and in each ch sp around, join in beg sc. *(8 petals)*

Rnd 4: Ch 1, working behind petals, fpsc around first sc on rnd 2, ch 4, [fpsc around next sc on rnd 2, ch 4] around, join in beg fpsc.

Rnd 5: Ch 1, (sc, 7 dc, sc) in first ch sp and in each ch sp around, join in beg sc.

Rnd 6: Ch 1, working behind petals, fpsc around first sc on rnd 4, ch 5, [fpsc around next sc on rnd 4, ch 5] around, join in beg fpsc.

Rnd 7: Sl st in first ch sp, ch 1, (sc, 5 dc) in same ch sp, ch 1, sc in first ch-3 picot on Edging of Center Rose Motif that will have you working toward ch-3 picot above Leaf point joining, work following steps to complete rnd:

A. Ch 1, sl st in last dc, (4 dc, sc) in same ch sp as last dc, (sc, 5 dc) in next ch-5 sp, ch 1, sk next ch-3 picot on Edging above Leaf point joining;

B. sc in next ch-3 picot on Edging of Center Rose Motif, ch 1, sl st in last dc, (4 dc, sc) in same ch sp;

C. (sc, 9 dc, sc) in next ch-5 sp, (sc, 5 dc) in next ch-5 sp, ch 1, sc in next ch-3 picot on next Arch on outside Motif, ch 1, sl st in last dc;

D. (4 dc, sc) in same ch sp as last dc, (sc, 9 dc, sc) in each of next 2 ch-5 sps, (sc, 5 dc) in next ch-5 sp, ch 1, sc in next ch-3 picot on next Arch on outside Motif, ch 1, sl st in last dc;

E. (4 dc, sc) in same ch sp as last dc, (sc, 9 dc, sc) in next ch-5 sp, join in beg sc. Fasten off.

2ND–6TH FILL-IN ROSES

Rep First Fill-In Rose in each open sp around Center Motif.

Block. ∎

Irish Rover
Scarf

SKILL LEVEL

INTERMEDIATE

FINISHED SIZE

6½ inches wide x 65 inches long,
excluding Fringe

MATERIALS

- NaturallyCaron.com Spa light
  (light worsted) weight yarn
  (3 oz/251 yds/ 85g per skein):
  2 skeins #0005 ocean spray
- Size F/5/3.75mm crochet hook
  or size needed to obtain gauge
- Stitch marker

GAUGE

Motif = 4½ inches across

PATTERN NOTES

Join with slip stitch as indicated unless
otherwise stated.

Weave in loose ends as work progresses.

SPECIAL STITCHES

Triple picot: Ch 4, sl st in front lp and
front strand of last st worked, ch 5, sl st
in same st, catching front lp of first ch
of beg ch-4, ch 4, sl st in same st,
catching front lp of beg ch-4
and ch-5.

Chain-3 picot (ch-3 picot): Ch 3,
sl st in top of last st worked.

INSTRUCTIONS
SCARF
FIRST MOTIF
Rnd 1: Ch 8, sl st in first ch to form ring, ch 1, 12 sc in ring, **join** (see Pattern Notes) in beg sc. (12 sc)

Rnd 2: Working in **front lps** (see Stitch Guide), ch 1, sc in first st, ch 3, [sc in next st, ch 3] around, join in beg sc. (12 ch sps, 12 sc)

Rnd 3: Working in **back lps** (see Stitch Guide) of rnd 1, ch 1, sc in first st, (sc, ch 9, sc) in next st, [sc in next st, (sc, ch 9, sc) in next st] around, join in beg sc.

Rnd 4: Ch 1, sc in first st, *ch 1, sk next st, (sc, ch 1, hdc, ch 1, {dc, ch 2} 3 times, dc, ch 1, hdc, ch 1, sc) in next ch-9 sp, ch 1, sk next sc**, sc in next st, rep from * around, ending last rep at **, join in beg sc.

Rnd 5: Sl st in first ch-1 sp and in next sc, ch 1, *2 sc in next ch-1 sp, (sc, ch 2, sc) in next ch sp, (2 sc, **ch-3 picot**—see Special Stitches, 2 sc) in each of next 3 ch-2 sps, (sc, ch 1, sc) in next ch-1 sp, 2 sc in next ch sp**, sk next 2 ch-1 sps, rep from * around, ending last rep at **, sc in last ch-1 sp, join in 2nd sl st. Fasten off.

2ND MOTIF
Rnds 1–4: Rep rnds 1–4 of First Motif.

Rnd 5: Sl st in first ch-1 sp and in next sc, ch 1, work the following steps to complete rnd:

A. *2 sc in next ch-1 sp, (sc, ch 2, sc) in next ch sp, (2 sc, ch-3 picot, 2 sc) in each of next 3 ch-2 sps, (sc, ch 1, sc) in next ch-1 sp;

B. 2 sc in next ch sp**, **sc dec** (see Stitch Guide) in next 2 ch-1 sps, 2 sc in next ch-1 sp, (sc, ch 2, sc) in next ch-1 sp;

C. (2 sc, ch 3-picot, 2 sc) in next ch-2 sp, 2 sc in next ch-2 sp, ch 1, sl st in center ch-3 picot on any petal of previous Motif, ch 1, (sl st, sc) in same ch-2 sp as last sc;

D. 2 sc in next ch-2 sp, ch 1, sl st in next ch-3 picot on same petal of previous Motif, ch 1, (sl st, sc) in same ch sp as last sc;

E. (sc, ch 2, sc) in next ch-1 sp, 2 sc in next ch-1 sp, sc dec next 2 ch-1 sps, 2 sc in next ch-1 sp, (sc, ch 2, sc) in next ch-1 sp;

F. 2 sc in next ch-2 sp, ch 1, sl st in first ch-3 picot on next petal of previous Motif, ch 1, (sl st, sc) in same ch sp as last sc;

G. 2 sc in next ch-2 sp, ch 1, sl st in center ch-3 picot of same petal, ch 1, (sl st, sc) in same ch sp as last sc;

H. (2 sc, ch-3 picot, 2 sc) in next ch-2 sp, (sc, ch 2, sc) in next ch-1 sp, 2 sc in next ch-1 sp, sc in last ch-1 sp, join in 2nd sl st at ch-1 sp. Fasten off.

3RD–15TH MOTIFS
Work same as 2nd Motif, joining to last Motif so there will be 1 free petal between joined petals.

EDGING
Rnd 1: Working across first long edge, join in first ch-3 picot on first free petal on side of Scarf that will have you working down the long side, work the following steps to complete rnd:

A. Ch 7, *sc in next ch-3 picot, ch 4, dc in next ch-3 picot, ch 4, dc in next ch-3 picot on next petal, ch 4, dc over joining between Motifs;

B. ch 4, [dc in next ch-3 picot on next petal, ch 4] twice, rep from * 13 times, sc in next ch-3 picot;

C. working around end, ch 4, [dc in next ch-3 picot on this petal, ch 4, dc in next ch-3 picot on next petal, ch 4, sc in next ch-3 picot, ch 4] 3 times;

D. working across rem long edge, **dc in next ch-3 picot, ch 4, dc in next ch-3 picot on next petal, ch 4, dc over joining between Motifs;

E. ch 4, [dc in next ch-3 picot on next petal, ch 4] twice, sc in next ch-3 picot, ch 4, rep from ** 13 times;

F. working around rem end, [dc in next ch-3 picot on this petal, ch 4, dc in next ch-3 picot on next petal, ch 4, sc in next ch-3 picot, ch 4] twice, dc in next ch-3 picot on this petal, ch 4, join in 3rd ch of beg ch-7.

Rnd 2: Working across first long edge, ch 1, 5 sc in first ch-4 sp, sc in next sc, 4 sc in next ch-4 sp, work the following steps to complete rnd:

A. *Ch 3, turn, (dc, ch 2, dc) in sc above ch-3 picot, ch 3, sk next 3 sc, sc in next sc, sl st in next sc, turn;

B. ch 1, (3 sc, ch-3 picot, 2 sc) in next ch-3 sp, (2 sc, ch-3 picot, sc) in next ch-2 sp, (3 sc, ch-3 picot, 2 sc) in next ch sp, sc in same ch-4 sp;

C. (3 sc, **triple picot**—*see Special Stitches*, 2 sc) in next ch-4 sp, 5 sc in next ch-4 sp, sc in next dc, 3 sc in next ch-4 sp, turn;

D. ch 2, dc in sc above dc at joining, ch 2, sk next 2 sc, sc in next sc, sl st in next sc, turn;

E. ch 1, (2 sc, ch-3 picot, sc) in next ch-2 sp, sc in next dc, ch-3 picot, (2 sc, ch-3 picot, sc) in next ch-2 sp, 2 sc in same ch-4 sp on rnd 1;

F. (3 sc, triple picot, 2 sc) in next ch-4 sp, 5 sc in next ch-4 sp, sc in next sc, 4 sc in next ch-4 sp, rep from * in step A 13 times, ch 3, turn;

G. (dc, ch 2, dc) in sc above ch-3 picot, ch 3, sk next 3 sc, sc in next sc, sl st in next sc, turn;

H. ch 1, (3 sc, ch-3 picot, 2 sc) in next ch-3 sp, (2 sc, ch-3 picot, sc) in next ch-2 sp, (3 sc, ch-3 picot, 2 sc) in next ch sp, sc in same ch-4 sp worked in;

I. working around end, [3 sc in next ch-4 sp, ch 28, mark 15th ch, 3 sc in back lp of 2nd ch from hook, 3 sc in back lp of each of next 12 chs;

J. (2 sc, sl st) in next ch, 20 sc, working over rem ch, 3 sc in same ch sp on rnd 1] 7 times;

K. working across rem long edge, 5 sc in next ch-4 sp, sc in next sc, 4 sc in next ch-4 sp;

L. **ch 3, turn, (dc, ch 2, dc) in sc above ch-3 picot, ch 3, sk next 3 sc, sc in next sc, sl st in next sc, turn;

M. ch 1, (3 sc, ch-3 picot, 2 sc) in next ch-3 sp, (2 sc, ch-3 picot, sc) in next ch-2 sp, (3 sc,

ch-3 picot, 2 sc) in next ch sp, sc in same ch-4 sp on rnd 1, (3 sc, triple picot, 2 sc) in next ch-4 sp, 5 sc in next ch-4 sp, sc in next dc, 3 sc in next ch-4 sp, turn;

N. ch 2, dc in sc above dc at joining, ch 2, sk next 2 sc, sc in next sc, sl st in next sc, turn;

O. ch 1, (2 sc, ch-3 picot, sc) in next ch-2 sp, sc in next dc, ch-3 picot, (2 sc, ch-3 picot, sc) in next ch-3 sp, 2 sc in same ch-4 sp on rnd 1;

P. (3 sc, triple picot, 2 sc) in next ch-4 sp, 5 sc in next ch-4 sp, sc in next sc, 4 sc in next ch-4 sp, rep from ** in step L 13 times, ch 3, turn;

Q. (dc, ch 2, dc) in sc above ch-3 picot, ch 3, sk next 3 sc, sc in next sc, sl st in next sc, turn;

R. ch 1, (3 sc, ch-3 picot, 2 sc) in next ch-3 sp, (2 sc, ch-3 picot, sc) in next ch-2 sp, (3 sc, ch-3 picot, 2 sc) in next ch sp, sc in same ch-4 sp on rnd 1;

S. working around end, [3 sc in next ch-4 sp, ch 28, mark 15th ch, 3 sc in back lp of 2nd ch from hook, 3 sc in back lp of each of next 12 chs, (2 sc, sl st) in next ch, 20 sc working over rem ch, 3 sc in same ch sp on rnd 1] 7 times, join in beg sc. Fasten off. ∎

Trefoil
Doily

SKILL LEVEL

EXPERIENCED

FINISHED SIZE
13½ inches across at widest point

MATERIALS
- Size 10 crochet cotton:
  350 yds white
- Size 7/1.65mm steel crochet hook
  or size needed to obtain gauge

GAUGE
Rnds 1–3 = 1½ inches across

PATTERN NOTES
Join with slip stitch as indicated unless
otherwise stated.

Chain-2 at beginning of row or round counts as
first double crochet unless otherwise stated.

Weave in loose ends as work progresses.

SPECIAL STITCHES
Triple picot: Ch 4, sl st in front lp and front
strand of last st worked, ch 5, sl st in same st,
catching front lp of first ch of beg ch-4, ch 4,
sl st in same st, catching front lp of beg ch-4
and ch-5.

Chain-3 picot (ch-3 picot): Ch 3, sl st in top
of last st worked.

INSTRUCTIONS
DOILY
Rnd 1: Ch 7, sl st in first ch to form ring, **ch 2**
(see Pattern Notes), 23 dc in ring, **join** *(see
Pattern Notes)* in 2nd ch of beg ch-3. *(24 dc)*

Rnd 2: Ch 1, sc in first st, *ch 4, sk next st, sc in
next st**, [ch 2, sk next st, sc in next st] 3 times,
rep from * around, ending last rep at **, [ch 2, sk
next st, sc in next st] twice, ch 2, join in beg sc.

FIRST SHAMROCK
Row 3: Now working in rows, ch 1, 3 sc in first
ch sp, ch 12, sl st in 12th ch from hook to form
ring, ch 1, 4 sc in ring, **ch-3 picot** *(see Special
Stitches)*, [sc in ring, ch-3 picot] twice, *4 sc
in ring, ch-3 picot, [sc in ring, ch-3 picot]
twice, rep from * once, 3 sc in ring, sl st in
ring joining, turn, work the following steps to
complete row:

A. Sl st in 2nd sc in ring, ch 1, sc in same sc, [ch
10, sk next 5 sc, sc in next sc] 3 times, sl st in
next sc, turn;

B. ch 1, (sc, hdc, 12 dc, hdc, sc) in first ch-10
sp and in each ch-10 sp across, sl st in next
sc, turn;

C. ch 1, sc in first st, *[ch 6, sk next 4 sts, sc in
next st] twice, ch 6, sk next 4 sts, **sc dec** *(see
Stitch Guide)* in next 2 sts, rep from * once,
[ch 6, sk next 4 sts, sc in next st] 3 times, turn;

D. ch 1, (2 sc, {ch 3, 2 sc} 3 times) in first ch-6
sp and in each ch-6 sp across, sl st up to and
into the ring joining, 3 sc in same ch-4 sp on
this row, 3 sc in each of next 3 ch-2 sps, 3 sc in
next ch-4 sp.

2ND SHAMROCK

Row 3: Ch 12, sl st in 12th ch from hook to form ring, ch 1, 4 sc in ring, ch-3 picot, [sc in ring, ch-3 picot] twice, *4 sc in ring, ch-3 picot, [sc in ring, ch-3 picot] twice, rep from * once, 3 sc in ring, sl st in ring joining, turn:

Rep steps A–C of First Shamrock;

   D. ch 1, (2 sc, ch 3, 2 sc) in next ch-6 sp, ch 1, sl st in 2nd ch-3 sp on last ch-6 on First Shamrock, ch 1, (2 sc, ch 3, 2 sc) in same ch sp as last sc, (2 sc, {ch 3, 2 sc} 3 times) in each of next 8 ch-6 sps, sl st up to and into ring joining, 3 sc in next ch-4 sp, 3 sc in each of next 3 ch-2 sps, 3 sc in next ch-4 sp.

3RD SHAMROCK

Row 3: Ch 12, sl st in 12th ch from hook to form ring, ch 1, 4 sc in ring, ch-3 picot, [sc in ring, ch-3 picot] twice, *4 sc in ring, ch-3 picot, [sc in ring, ch-3 picot] twice, rep from * once, 3 sc in ring, sl st in ring joining, turn:

Rep steps A–C of First Shamrock;

D. ch 1, (2 sc, ch 3, 2 sc) in next ch-6 sp, ch 1, sl st in 2nd ch-3 sp on last ch-6 on 2nd Shamrock, ch 1, (2 sc, ch 3, 2 sc) in same ch sp as last sc, (2 sc, {ch 3, 2 sc} 3 times) in each of next 7 ch-6 sps, (2 sc, ch 3, 2 sc) in next ch-6 sp, ch 1, sl st in 2nd ch-3 sp on first ch-6 sp of First Shamrock, ch 1, (2 sc, ch 3, 2 sc) in same ch sp as last sc, sl st up to and into ring joining, 3 sc in next ch-4 sp on this row, 3 sc in each of last 3 ch-2 sps, join in beg sc. Fasten off.

EDGING

Rnd 1: Join in first ch-3 sp on 5th ch-6 sp of any Shamrock, ch 12, sk next ch-3 sp, *tr in next ch-3 sp, ch 5, sk next ch-3 sp, dc in next ch-3 sp, ch 5, sk next 2 ch-3 sps, dc in next ch-3 sp, ch 7, sk next 2 ch-3 sps, tr in next ch-3 sp, ch 5, sk next 4 ch-3 sps, tr in next ch-3 sp, ch 7, sk next 2 ch-3 sps, dc in next ch-3 sp, ch 5, sk next 2 ch-3 sps, dc in next ch-3 sp, ch 5, sk next ch-3 sp**, tr in next ch-3 sp, ch 9, sk next ch-3 sp, rep from * around, ending last rep at **, join in 3rd ch of beg ch-12.

Rnd 2: Sl st in first ch-9 sp, ch 2, (4 dc, 5 tr, 5 dc) in same ch sp, *7 dc in each of next 2 ch-5 sps, 9 dc in next ch-7 sp, 7 dc in next ch-5 sp, 9 dc in next ch-7 sp, 7 dc in each of next 2 ch-5 sps**, (5 dc, 5 tr, 5 dc) in next ch-9 sp, rep from * around, ending last rep at **, join in 2nd ch of beg ch-2.

Rnd 3: Ch 3 (*counts as first dc and ch-1*), sk next dc, dc in next dc, ch 1, sk next dc, dc in next dc, *ch 1, sk next tr, dc in next tr, ch 1, (dc, ch 3, dc) in next tr, ch 1, dc in next tr, ch 1, sk next tr, dc in next dc, [ch 1, sk next dc, dc in next dc] 31 times, rep from * once, ch 1, sk next tr, dc in next tr, ch 1, (dc, ch 3, dc) in next tr, ch 1, dc in next tr, ch 1, sk next tr, dc in next dc, [ch 1, sk next dc, dc in next dc] 29 times, ch 1, join in 2nd ch of beg ch-3.

Rnd 4: Sl st in first ch-1 sp, ch 1, 2 sc in same ch sp, 2 sc in each of next 3 ch-1 sps, work following steps to complete rnd:

A. 3 sc in next ch-3 sp, ch 12, sl st in 12th ch from hook to form ring, ch 1, 4 sc in ring, ch-3 picot, [sc in ring, ch-3 picot] twice, *4 sc in ring, ch-3 picot, [sc in ring, ch-3 picot] twice, rep from * once, 3 sc in ring, sl st in ring joining, turn; rep steps A–C of First Shamrock;

B. ch 1, 2 sc in first ch-6 sp, ch 1, sl st in 5th ch from beg of Shamrock, ch 1, (2 sc, {ch 3, 2 sc} twice) in same ch-6 sp, [(2 sc, {ch 3, 2 sc} 3 time) in next ch-6 sp] 8 times, sl st up to and into the ring joining, 3 sc in same ch-3 sp, 2 sc in next ch-1 sp, sl st in last ch-3 sp on Shamrock (*Shamrock completed*);

C. 2 sc in each of next 8 ch-1 sps, sc in next ch-1 sp, 2 sc in each of next 2 ch-1 sps, turn;

D. ch 1, sk next 3 sc, (tr, {ch 1, tr} 5 times) in next sc, ch 1, sk next 3 sc, sc in next sc, sl st in next sc, turn;

E. 2 sc in each of next 3 ch-1 sps, 3 sc in next ch-1 sp, 2 sc in each of next 3 ch-1 sps, sc in next ch-1 sp on rnd 6, turn;

F. ch 1, sc in first sc, ch 5, sk next 4 sc, sc in next sc, ch 5, sk next 3 sc, sc in next sc, ch 5, sk next 4 sc, sc in next sc, sl st in next sc, turn;

G. ch 1, (2 sc, {ch 3, 2 sc} 3 times) in each of next 2 ch-6 sps, (2 sc, ch 3, 2 sc, ch 5, 2 sc, ch 3, 2 sc) in next ch-6 sp, sc in same ch-1 sp on rnd 6, (*fan completed*);

H. 2 sc in each of next 4 ch-1 sps, sc in next ch-1 sp, 2 sc in each of next 2 ch-1 sps, sc in next ch-1 sp, turn;

I. ch 1, sk next 4 sc, (dtr, {ch 1, dtr} 7 times) in next st, ch 1, sk next 4 sts, sc in next st, sl st in next st, turn;

J. ch 1, 2 sc in each of next 4 ch-1 sps, sc in next ch-1 sp, rep steps A–C of First Shamrock;

K. ch 1, (2 sc, {ch 3, 2 sc} twice) in first ch-6 sp, ch 2, sl st in next ch-5 sp of first fan, ch 2, 2 sc in same ch-6 sp, (2 sc, {ch 3, 2 sc} 3 times) in each of next 7 ch-6 sps, (2 sc, ch 5, 2 sc, {ch 3, 2 sc} twice) in next ch-6 sp, sl st up to and into ring joining, sc in same ch-1 sp on fan, 2 sc in each of next 4 ch-1 sps, sc in next ch-1 sp on rnd 6;

L. 2 sc in each of next 4 ch-1 sps, sc in next ch-1 sp, 2 sc in each of next 2 ch-1 sps, turn;

M. ch 1, sk next 4 sc, (tr, {ch 1, tr} 5 times) in next sc, ch 1, sk next 3 sc, sc in next sc, sl st in next sc, turn;

N. rep steps E and F;

O. (2 sc, ch 3, 2 sc) in next ch-6 sp, ch 2, sl st in ch-5 sp on Shamrock, ch 2, (2 sc, ch 3, 2 sc) in same ch-6 sp, (2 sc, {ch 3, 2 sc} 3 times) in each of next 2 ch-6 sps, sc in same ch-1 sp on rnd 6;

P. 2 sc in each of next 6 ch-1 sps;

Q. rep steps A–P once, rep steps A–O once;

R. sc in same ch-1 sp on rnd 6, 2 sc in each of last 2 ch-1 sps, join in beg sc.

FIRST POINT EDGING

Row 1: With RS facing, join in first sc at 4th ch-1 sp from tip of Shamrock at corner of Doily, ch 6, sk first ch-3 sp on fan, dc in next ch-3 sp, ch 6, sk next 2 ch-3 sps, tr in next ch-3 sp, ch 6, sk next 3 ch-3 sps, tr in next ch-3 sp, [ch 6, sk next 2 ch-3 sps, dc in next ch-3 sp] 3 times, ch 4, dc in same ch sp, [ch 6, sk next 2 ch-3 sps, dc in next ch-3 sp] twice, ch 6, sk next 2 ch-3 sps, tr in next ch-3 sp, ch 6, sk next 3 ch-3 sps, tr in next ch-3 sp, ch 6, sk next 2 ch-3 sps, dc in next ch-3 sp, ch 6, sc in 2nd sc at 3rd ch-1 sp from fan, sl st in each of next 2 sts, turn.

Row 2: Ch 3, (dc, ch 3, dc) in next ch-6 sp, [ch 3, (dc, ch 3, dc) in next ch-6 sp] 5 times, ch 4, (dc, ch 4, dc) in next ch-4 sp, ch 4, (dc, ch 3, dc) in next ch-6 sp, [ch 3, (dc, ch 3, dc) in next ch-6 sp] 5 times, ch 3, sk next sc on Doily, sc in next sc, sl st in next sc, turn.

Row 3: Ch 1, 4 sc in next ch-3 sp, sl st in 2nd ch-3 sp on petal of Shamrock, 4 sc in next ch-3 sp, 3 sc in each of next 2 ch-3 sps, ch 3, turn, work following steps to complete row:

A. Ch 3, sk next 3 sc, (dc, ch 3, dc) in next sc, ch 3, sk next 3 sc, sc in next sc, turn;

B. (2 sc, ch 3, 2 sc) in first ch-3 sp, 2 sc in next ch-3 sp, **triple picot** (see Special Stitches), 2 sc in same ch sp, (2 sc, ch 3, 2 sc) in next ch-3 sp, 2 sc in same ch-3 sp on row 2, 4 sc in next ch-3 sp, 3 sc in each of next 2 ch-3 sps, turn;

C. rep steps A, B and A;

D. (2 sc, ch 3, 2 sc) in first ch-3 sp, (2 sc, triple picot, 2 sc) in next ch-3 sp, (2 sc, ch 3, 2 sc) in next ch-3 sp, 2 sc in same ch-3 sp on this row, 4 sc in next ch-3 sp, 3 sc in next ch-3 sp, 3 sc in next ch-4 sp;

E. ch 3, sk next 3 sc, (dc, ch 3, dc) in next sc, ch 3, sk next 3 sc, sc in next sc, turn;

F. ch 1, (2 sc, ch 3, 2 sc) in next ch-3 sp, (2 sc, triple picot, 2 sc) in next ch-3 sp, (2 sc, ch 3, 2 sc) in next ch-3 sp, 2 sc in same ch-4 sp on row 2, 5 sc in next ch-4 sp, 2 sc in next ch-4 sp, turn;

G. ch 3, sk next 3 sc, (dc, ch 3, dc) in next sc, ch 3, sk next 3 sc, sc in next sc, turn;

H. ch 1, (2 sc, ch 3, 2 sc) in first ch-3 sp, (2 sc, triple picot, 2 sc) in next ch-3 sp, (2 sc, ch 3, 2 sc) in next ch-3 sp, sc in same ch-3 sp on row 2, *4 sc in next ch-3 sp, 3 sc in each of next 2 ch-3 sps, turn;

I. ch 3, sk next 3 sc, (dc, ch 3, dc) in next sc, ch 3, sk next 3 sc, sc in next sc, turn;

J. ch 1, (2 sc, ch 3, 2 sc) in next ch-3 sp, (2 sc, triple picot, 2 sc) in next ch-3 sp, (2 sc, ch 3, 2 sc) in next ch-3 sp, sc in same ch-3 sp on row 2;

K. rep from * in step H 3 times, sl st in first ch-3 sp on petal of Shamrock, 4 sc in next ch-3 sp, sl st in next sc on Doily. Fasten off.

2ND & 3RD POINT EDGINGS
Work same as First Point Edging. ∎

April Morn
Shawl

SKILL LEVEL

■■■■

EXPERIENCED

FINISHED SIZE

45 inches long x 60 inches wide

MATERIALS

- Red Heart Luster Sheen fine (sport) weight yarn (4 oz/335 yds/ 113g per skein):
  8 skeins #332 tan
- Size D/3/3.25mm crochet hook or size needed to obtain gauge
- Mini fine-point marker
- Stitch markers

2 FINE

GAUGE

Shamrock Motif = 6 inches per side

PATTERN NOTES

Join with slip stitch as indicated unless otherwise stated.

When making padding-cord ring, do not wrap it too tightly or you will have trouble sliding lps off and retaining its shape. Leave about 1-inch end at beginning and end of wrap. This will make it a little easier to handle.

Work your ends in as you go so you won't have a major job at the end.

SPECIAL STITCHES

Padded ring: Leaving 1-inch end (*see Pattern Notes*), wrap yarn around nonworking end of mini fine-point marker number of times stated in instructions, leavening 1 inch end, fasten off. Gently slide lps off hook and insert hook in ring, yo, pull lp through, yo, pull through both lps on hook (*sc*).

Extended double crochet (ext dc): Yo, insert hook as indicated in instructions, yo, pull through 1 lp on hook, [yo, pull through 2 lps on hook] twice.

Chain-3 picot (ch-3 picot): Ch 3, sl st in top of last st worked.

Extended double crochet decrease (ext dc dec): Holding back last lp of each st on hook, ext dc as indicated in instructions, yo, pull through all lps on hook.

Joining picot: Ch 1, sl st in corresponding ch-3 picot on previous Motif, ch 1, sl st in top of last sc worked.

Chain-5 picot (ch-5 picot): Ch 5, sl st in top of last st worked.

Chain-5 picot chain (ch-5 picot ch): [Ch 5, sl st in 4th ch from hook] twice, ch 2.

Chain-7 picot (ch-7 picot): Ch 7, sl st in top of last st worked.

INSTRUCTIONS

SHAWL
FIRST SHAMROCK MOTIF

Rnd 1: Using the bottom end of mini marker, work **padded ring** (*see Special Stitches*) wrapping 12 times, [8 sc in ring, **ch-3 picot** (*see Special Stitches*)] 3 times, **join** (*see Pattern Notes*) in beg sc. (*3 picots, 24 sc*)

Rnd 2: Ch 1, sk first st, sc in each of next 5 sts, ch 10, sk next 3 sts, [sc in each of next 5 sts, ch 10, sk next 3 sts] twice, join in beg sc. *(3 petals)*

Rnd 3: Ch 1, sk first st, [sc in each of next 3 sts, ch 1, (sc, ch 1, hdc, ch 1, dc, {ch 2, tr} 4 times, ch 2, dc, ch 1, hdc, ch 1, sc) in next ch-10 sp, ch 1] around, join in beg sc.

Rnd 4: Ch 1, sk first st, (sc, ch-3 picot, sc) in next st, ch 1, sc in 2nd ch-1 sp on petal, (sc, ch-3 picot, sc) in next ch-1 sp, (2 sc, ch-3 picot, sc) in each of next 5 ch-2 sps, (sc, ch-3 picot, sc) in next ch-1 sp, sc in next ch-1 sp, ch 1, sk next st, next ch sp and next st, *(sc, ch-3 picot, sc) in next st, ch 1, sc in 2nd ch-1 sp on petal, (sc, ch 3-picot, sc) in next ch-1 sp, (2 sc, ch-3 picot, sc) in each of next 5 ch-2 sps, (sc, ch-3 picot) in next ch-1 sp, sc in next ch-1 sp, ch 1, sk next sc, next ch sp** and next sc, rep from * around ending last rep at **, join in beg sc. Fasten off.

Rnd 5: Join in 4th ch-3 picot on any petal, (ch 6, tr, ch 3, **ext dc**—*see Special Stitches*) in same ch-3 picot, *ch 4, sc in next ch-3 picot, ch 4, hdc in next ch-3 picot, ch 4, **ext dc dec** *(see Special Stitches)* in next ch-3 picot, sk next ch-3 picot and in next ch-3 picot, ch 4, hdc in next ch-3 picot, ch 4, sc in next ch-3 picot, ch 4**, (ext dc, ch 3, tr, ch 3, ext dc) in next ch-3 picot, rep from * around, ending last rep at **, join in 3rd ch of beg ch-6.

Rnd 6: Ch 1, sc in first st, *ch-3 picot, 3 sc in next ch sp, sc in next tr, ch 7, sl st in top of last sc worked, 3 sc in next ch-3 sp, sc in next ext dc, ch-3 picot, 4 sc in next ch-4 sp, sc in next sc, ch-3 picot, 4 sc in next ch-4 sp, sc in next hdc, ch-3 picot, 4 sc in next ch-4 sp, sc in sp between sts of ext dc dec, ch-3 picot, 4 sc in next ch-4 sp, sc in next hdc, ch-3 picot, 4 sc in next ch-4 sp, sc in next sc, ch 3-picot, 4 sc in next ch-4 sp**, sc in next ext dc, rep from * around, ending last rep at **, join in beg sc. Fasten off.

2ND SHAMROCK MOTIF
Rnds 1–5: Rep rnds 1–5 of First Shamrock Motif.

Rnd 6: Ch 1, sc in first st, ch-3 picot, 3 sc in next ch sp, sc in next tr, ch 7, sl st in top of last sc worked, work the following steps to complete rnd:

A. 3 sc in next ch-3 sp, sc in next ext dc, ch-3 picot;

B. *4 sc in next ch-4 sp, sc in next sc, ch-3 picot, 4 sc in next ch-4 sp, sc in next hdc, ch-3 picot, 4 sc in next ch-4 sp;

C. sc in sp between sts of ext dc dec, ch-3 picot, 4 sc in next ch-4 sp, sc in next hdc, ch-3 picot, 4 sc in next ch-4 sp, sc in next sc, ch-3 picot, 4 sc in next ch-4 sp**;

D. sc in next ext dc, ch 3-picot, 3 sc in next ch-3 sp, ch 3, sl st in ch-7 sp on previous Motif;

E. ch 3, sl st in top of last sc worked, 3 sc in next ch-3 sp , sc in next ext dc, **joining picot** (see Special Stitches), 4 sc in next ch-4 sp, sc in next sc, joining picot;

F. 4 sc in next ch-4 sp, sc in next hdc, joining picot, 4 sc in next ch-4 sp, sc in sp between sts of next ext dc dec, joining picot, 4 sc in next ch-4 sp, sc in next hdc, joining picot;

G. 4 sc in next ch-4 sp, sc in next sc, joining picot, 4 sc in next ch-4 sp, sc in next ext dc, joining picot;

H. 3 sc in next ch-3 sp, sc in next tr, ch 3, sl st in next ch-7 sp on previous Motif, ch 3, sl st in top of last sc worked, 3 sc in next ch-3 sp, sc in next ext dc, ch-3 picot, rep from * in step B around, ending last rep at ** in step C, join in beg sc. Fasten off.

3RD & 4TH SHAMROCK MOTIFS
Rep 2nd Shamrock Motif on each side of First Shamrock Motif.

TRIANGLE EDGING
Rnd 1: Join in any open ch-7 sp on top corner of Triangle, ch 4, (dc {ch 2, dc} 4 times) in same ch sp, *ch 4, [dc in next ch-3 picot, ch 4] 7 times, ext dc in base of ch-7 sp on same Shamrock Motif, ch 4, ext dc in center of next ch-7 sp on next Shamrock Motif, ch 4, ext dc in base of next ch-7 sp on next Shamrock Motif, ch 4, [dc in next ch-3 picot, ch 4] 7 times**, (dc, {ch 2, dc} 5 times) in next ch-7 sp, rep from * around, ending last rep at **, join in 2nd ch of beg ch 4.

Rnd 2: Ch 1, sc in first st, [2 sc in next ch-2 sp, sc in next dc] twice, 3 sc in next ch-2 sp, sc in next dc, [2 sc in next ch-2 sp, sc in next dc] twice, 5 sc in each of next 18 ch-4 sps, *[sc in next dc, 2 sc in next ch-2 sp] twice, sc in next dc, 3 sc in next ch-2 sp, sc in next dc, [2 sc in next ch-2 sp, sc in next dc] twice, 5 sc in each of next 18 ch-4 sps, rep from * around, join in beg sc. Fasten off.

FIRST PICOT ROWS
Row 1: Join with sc in center sc of 3-sc group in corner, **ch-5 picot ch** (see Special Stitches), sk next 4 sc, sc in next sc, ch-5 picot ch, sk next 5 sc, sc in next sc, [ch-5 picot ch, sk next 4 sts, sc in next sc] 19 times, ch-5 picot ch, sk next sc, sc in next sc, [ch-5 picot ch, sk next 4 sc, sc in next sc] 19 times, ch-5 picot ch, sk next 5 sc, sc in next sc, ch-5 picot ch, sk next 4 sc, sc in next sc, leaving rem sts unworked, turn. (21 ch-5 picot chs on each side with 1 at point)

Row 2: Ch 1, sc in first st, ch 9, sl st in 4th ch from hook, ch 2, sc in ch sp between next 2 picots, [ch-5 picot ch, sc in ch sp between next 2 picots] 21 times, ch-5 picot ch, sc in same ch sp, [ch-5 picot ch, sc in ch sp between next 2 picots] 21 times, ch-5 picot ch, join with dtr in last st, forming last ch sp, turn.

Row 3: Ch 1, sc last ch sp, [ch-5 picot ch, sc in ch sp between next 2 picots] 22 times, ch-5 picot ch, sc in same ch sp, [ch-5 picot ch, sc in next ch sp between picots] 21 times, ch-5 picot ch, sc in ch sp after next picot, turn.

Row 4: Ch 1, sc in first st, ch 9, sc in ch sp between next 2 picots, ch 6, sc in ch sp between next 2 picots, ch 6, sl st in 4th ch from hook, ch 3, sc in ch sp between next 2 picot, *[ch 6, sc in ch sp between next 2 picots] twice, ch 6, sl st in 4th ch from hook, ch 3, sc in next ch sp between next 2 picots, rep from * 5 times, [ch 6, sc in ch sp between next 2 picots] twice, ch 7, sc in same ch sp, **[ch 6, sc in ch sp between next 2 picots] twice, ch 6, sl st in 4th ch from hook, ch 3, sc in sp between next 2 picots, rep from ** 6 times, ch 6, sc in next ch sp between picots, ch 9, sc in last st. Fasten off.

FIRST ROW OF ROSES
FIRST ROSE
Rnd 1: Ch 6, sl st in first ch to form ring, ch 1, 12 sc in ring, join in beg sc. (12 sc)

Rnd 2: Ch 1, sc in first st, ch 3, sk next st, [sc in next st, ch 3, sk next st] around, join in beg sc. (6 ch sps)

Rnd 3: Ch 1, (sc, 5 dc, sc) in first ch sp and in each ch sp around, join in beg sc. (6 petals)

Rnd 4: Working behind petals, fpsc (see Stitch Guide) around sc on rnd 2, ch 4, [fpsc around next sc on rnd 2, ch 4] around, join in beg fpsc.

Rnd 5: Ch 1, (sc, 7 dc, sc) in first ch sp and in each of next 3 ch sps, (sc, 4 dc) in next ch sp, with Rose facing Shawl, sl st in ch-9 st at beg of row 4 on First Picot Rows, (3 dc, sc) in same ch sp on Rose, (sc, 4 dc) in next ch sp, sl st in next ch-6 sp on row 4 of First Picot Rows, (3 dc, sc) in same ch sp on Rose, join in beg sc. Fasten off.

2ND–8TH ROSES
Rnds 1–4: Rep rnds 1–4 of First Rose.

Rnd 5: Ch 1, (sc, 7 dc, sc) in first ch sp and in each of next 2 ch sps, (sc, 4 dc) in next ch sp, with Rose facing Shawl, sl st in 4th dc of petal of Rose closest to Shawl that will have you working toward Shawl, (3 dc, sc) in same ch sp on Rose, (sc, 4 dc) in next ch sp, sk ch sp with picot on Shawl, sl st in next ch-6 sp on Shawl, (3 dc, sc) in same ch sp on Rose, (sc, 4 dc) in next ch sp, sl st in next ch-6 sp on Shawl, (3 dc, sc) in same ch sp on Rose, join in beg sc. Fasten off.

9TH ROSE
Rnds 1–4: Rep rnds 1–4 of First Rose.

Rnd 5: Ch 1, (sc, 7 dc, sc) in first ch sp and in each of next 3 ch sps, (sc, 4 dc) in next ch sp, sl st in 4th dc of petal of 8th Rose, (3 dc, sc) in same ch sp on this Rose, (sc, 4 dc) in next ch sp, sl st in next ch-7 sp on point of Shawl, (3 dc, sc) in same ch sp on this Rose, join in beg sc. Fasten off.

10TH ROSE
Rnds 1–4: Rep rnds 1–4 of First Rose.

Rnd 5: Ch 1, (sc, 7 dc, sc) in first ch sp and in each of next 2 ch sps, (sc, 4 dc) in next ch sp, sl st in 4th dc of petal on 9th Rose, (3 dc, sc) in same ch sp on this Rose, *(sc, 4 dc) in next ch sp, sl st in next ch-6 sp on Shawl, (3 dc, sc) in same ch sp on this Rose, rep from * once, join in beg sc. Fasten off.

11TH–16TH ROSES
Rnds 1–4: Rep rnds 1–4 of First Rose.

Rnd 5: Ch 1, (sc, 7 dc, sc) in first ch sp and in each of next 2 ch sps, (sc, 4 dc) in next ch sp, with Rose facing Shawl, sl st in 4th dc of petal of Rose closest to Shawl that will have you working toward Shawl, (3 dc, sc) in same ch sp on Rose, (sc, 4 dc) in next ch sp, sk ch sp with picot on Shawl, sl st in next ch-6 sp on Shawl, (3 dc, sc) in same ch sp on Rose, (sc, 4 dc) in next ch sp, sl st in next ch-6 sp on Shawl, (3 dc, sc) in same ch sp on Rose, join in beg sc. Fasten off.

17TH ROSE
Rnds 1–4: Rep rnds 1–4 of First Rose.

Rnd 5: Ch 1, (sc, 7 dc, sc) in first ch sp and in each of next 2 ch sps, (sc, 4 dc) in next ch sp, with Rose facing Shawl, sl st in 4th dc of petal of Rose closest to Shawl that will have you working toward Shawl, (3 dc, sc) in same ch sp on Rose, (sc, 4 dc) in next ch sp, sk ch sp with picot on Shawl, sl st in next ch-6 sp on Shawl, (3 dc, sc) in same ch sp on Rose, (sc, 4 dc) in next ch sp, sl st in next ch-9 sp on Shawl, (3 dc, sc) in same ch sp on Rose, join in beg sc. Fasten off.

2ND PICOT ROWS
Row 1: With RS facing, join in 4th dc of first free petal on 17th Rose that will have you working toward next free petal of same Rose, ch 9, sc in 4th dc of next petal, ch 5, sc in 4th dc of next petal, [ch 6, sc in 4th dc of next petal on next Rose, ch 5, sc in 4th dc of next petal on same

Rose] 7 times, ch 6, dc in 4th dc on next petal on center Rose at point, ch 5, (tr, ch 5, dtr, ch 5, tr) in 4th dc on next petal, ch 5, dc in 4th dc of next petal, [ch 6, sc in 4th dc of next petal on next Rose, ch 5, sc in 4th dc of next petal on same Rose] 8 times, ch 4, dtr in 4th dc of next petal on last Rose, turn.

Row 2: Ch 1, (sc, ch-5 picot ch) 3 times in first ch sp, *[sc in next ch-5 sp, (ch-5 picot ch, sc) twice in next ch-6 sp, ch-5 picot ch] 8 times, sc in next ch-5 sp*, [(ch-5 picot ch, sc) twice in next ch-5 sp] twice, ch-5 picot ch, rep between * once, (ch-5 picot ch, sc) 3 times in last ch sp, turn.

Row 3: Ch 1, sc in first ch sp, ch 9, sl st in 4th ch from hook, ch 2, sc in ch sp between next 2 picots, [ch-5 picot ch, sc in ch sp between next 2 picots] 29 times, ch-5 picot ch, sc in same ch sp, [ch-5 picot ch, sc in ch sp between next 2 picots] 29 times, ch-5 picot ch, dtr in last st, turn.

Row 4: Ch 1, sc in first ch sp, ch 9, sl st in 4th ch from hook, ch 2, sc in ch sp between next 2 picots, [ch-5 picot ch, sc in ch sp between next 2 picots] 29 times, ch 5, sl st in 4th ch from hook, sc in same ch sp, [ch-5 picot ch, sc in ch sp between next 2 picots] 29 times, ch 5, sl st in 4th ch from hook, ch 2, dtr in last st, turn.

Row 5: Ch 7, dc in same ch sp, [ch-4, dc in ch sp between next 2 picots] 29 times, ch 4, (tr, ch 4, dtr, ch 4, tr) in ch sp between next 2 picots, [ch-4, dc in ch sp between next 2 picots] 29 times, ch 4, (dc, ch 4, tr) in ch sp after last picot on last ch sp, turn.

Row 6: Ch 1, sc in first st, **ch-5 picot** *(see Special Stitches)*, [4 sc in next ch-4 sp, sc in next dc, ch-3 picot] 30 times, 4 sc in next ch-4 sp, sc in next tr, ch-3 picot, 4 sc in next ch-4 sp, sc in next dtr, **ch-7 picot** *(see Special Stitches)*, 4 sc in next ch-4 sp, sc in next tr, ch-3 picot, [4 sc in next ch-4 sp, sc in next dc, ch-3 picot] 30 times, 5 sc in last ch-4 sp, ch-5 picot. Fasten off.

INNER SHAMROCK MOTIFS
FIRST INNER MOTIF
Rnds 1–5: Rep rnds 1–5 of First Shamrock Motif on pages 26 and 27.

Rnd 6: Ch 1, sc in first st, ch-3 picot, 3 sc in next ch-3 sp, sc in next tr, ch 7, sl st in top of last sc, work the following steps to complete rnd:

A. 3 sc in next ch-3 sp, sc in next ext dc, ch-3 picot, 4 sc in next ch-4 sp, sc in next sc, ch-3 picot, 4 sc in next ch-4 sp, sc in next hdc, ch-3 picot, 4 sc in next ch-4 sp, sc in sp between ext dc dec;

B. ch-3 picot, 4 sc in next ch-4 sp, sc in next hdc, ch-3 picot, 4 sc in next ch-4 sp, sc in next sc, ch-3 picot, 4 sc in next ch-4 sp, sc in next ext dc;

C. ch-3 picot, 3 sc in next ch-3 sp, sc in next tr, ch 3, sl st in ch-5 sp at end of row 6 of Shawl, ch 3, sl st in top of last sc worked, 3 sc in next ch-3 sp, sc in next ext dc, ch 1, sc in next picot on Shawl, ch 1, sl st in top of last sc worked;

D. 4 sc in next ch-4 sp, sc in next sc, ch 1, sc in next picot on Shawl, ch 1, sl st in top of last sc worked;

E. 4 sc in next ch-4 sp, sc in next hdc, ch 1, sc in next picot on Shawl, ch 1, sl st in top of last sc worked;

F. 4 sc in next ch-4 sp, sc in sp between ext dc dec, ch 1, sc in next picot on Shawl, ch 1, sl st in top of last sc worked;

G. 4 sc in next ch-4 sp, sc in next hdc, ch 1, sc in next picot on Shawl, ch 1, sl st in top of last sc worked;

H. 4 sc in next ch-4 sp, sc in next sc, ch 1, sc in next picot on Shawl, ch 1, sl st in top of last sc worked;

I. 4 sc in next ch-4 sp, sc in next ext dc, ch 1, sc in next picot on Shawl, ch 1, sl st in top of last sc worked;

J. 3 sc in next ch-3 sp, sc in next tr, ch 3, sl st in next picot on Shawl, ch 3, sl st in top of sc worked;

K. 3 sc in next ch-3 sp, sc in next ext dc, ch-3 picot, 4 sc in next ch-4 sp, sc in next sc, ch-3 picot;

L. 4 sc in next ch-4 sp, sc in next hdc, ch-3 picot, 4 sc in next ch-4 sp, sc in sp between ext dc dec, ch-3 picot, 4 sc in next ch-4 sp, sc in next hdc, ch-3 picot;

M. 4 sc in next ch-4 sp, sc in next sc, ch-3 picot, 4 sc in last ch-4 sp, join in beg sc. Fasten off.

2ND & 3RD INNER MOTIFS

Rnds 1–5: Rep rnds 1–5 of First Shamrock Motif on pages 26 and 27.

Rnd 6: Ch 1, sc in first st, ch-3 picot, 3 sc in next ch-3 sp, sc in next tr, ch 7, sl st in top of last sc worked, work the following steps to complete rnd:

A. 3 sc in next ch-3 sp, sc in next ext dc, ch-3 picot, 4 sc in next ch-4 sp, sc in next sc, ch-3 picot, 4 sc in next ch-4 sp, sc in next hdc, ch-3 picot, 4 sc in next ch-4 sp, sc in sp between ext dc dec;

B. ch-3 picot, 4 sc in next ch-4 sp, sc in next hdc, ch-3 picot, 4 sc in next ch-4 sp, sc in next sc, ch-3 picot, 4 sc in next ch-4 sp, sc in next ext dc;

C. ch-3 picot, 3 sc in next ch-3 sp, sc in next tr, ch 3, sl st in same picot on Shawl as last picot Motif joining of previous Motif, ch 3, sl st in top of last sc worked, 3 sc in next ch-3 sp, sc in next ext dc;

D. ch 1, sc in next picot on Shawl, ch 1, sl st in top of last sc worked, 4 sc in next ch-4 sp, sc in next sc;

E. ch 1, sc in next picot on Shawl, ch 1, sl st in top of last sc worked, 4 sc in next ch-4 sp, sc in next hdc;

F. ch 1, sc in next picot on Shawl, ch 1, sl st in top of last sc worked, 4 sc in next ch-4 sp, sc in sp between ext dc dec;

G. ch 1, sc in next picot on Shawl, ch 1, sl st in top of last sc worked, 4 sc in next ch-4 sp, sc in next hdc;

H. ch 1, sc in next picot on Shawl, ch 1, sl st in top of last sc worked, 4 sc in next ch-4 sp, sc in next sc;

I. ch 1, sc in next picot on Shawl, ch 1, sl st in top of last sc worked, 4 sc in next ch-4 sp, sc in next ext dc;

J. ch 1, sc in next picot on Shawl, ch 1, sl st in top of last sc worked, 3 sc in next ch-3 sp, sc in next tr;

K. ch 3, sl st in next picot on Shawl, ch 3, sl st in top of last sc worked, 3 sc in next ch-3 sp, sc in next ext dc;

L. ch-3 picot, 4 sc in next ch-4 sp, sc in next sc, ch-3 picot, 4 sc in next ch-4 sp, sc in next hdc, ch-3 picot, 4 sc in next ch-4 sp, sc in sp between ext dc dec;

M. ch-3 picot, 4 sc in next ch-4 sp, sc in next hdc, ch-3 picot, 4 sc in next ch-4 sp, sc in next sc, ch-3 picot, 4 sc in last ch-4 sp, join in beg sc. Fasten off.

4TH INNER MOTIF

Rnds 1–5: Rep rnds 1–5 of First Shamrock Motif on pages 26 and 27.

Rnd 6: Ch 1, sc in first st, ch-3 picot, 3 sc in next ch-3 sp, sc in next tr, ch 7, sl st in top of last sc worked, work the following steps to complete rnd:

A. 3 sc in next ch-3 sp, sc in next ext dc, ch-3 picot, 4 sc in next ch-4 sp, sc in next sc, ch-3 picot, 4 sc in next ch-4 sp, sc in next hdc, ch-3 picot, 4 sc in next ch-4 sp, sc in sp between ext dc dec;

B. ch-3 picot, 4 sc in next ch-4 sp, sc in next hdc, ch-3 picot, 4 sc in next ch-4 sp, sc in next sc, ch-3 picot, 4 sc in next ch-4 sp, sc in next ext dc;

C. ch-3 picot, 3 sc in next ch-3 sp, sc in next tr, ch 3, sl st in same picot on Shawl as last picot Motif joining of previous Motif;

D. ch 3, sl st in top of last sc worked, 3 sc in next ch-3 sp, sc in next ext dc, ch 1, sc in next picot on Shawl, ch 1, sl st in top of last sc worked;

E. 4 sc in next ch-4 sp, sc in next sc, ch 1, sc in next picot on Shawl, ch 1, sl st in top of last sc worked;

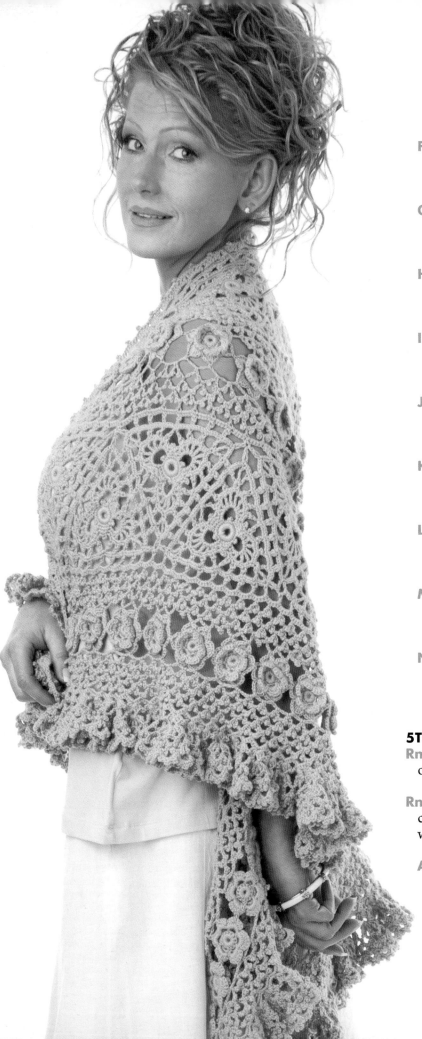

F. 4 sc in next ch-4 sp, sc in next hdc, ch 1, sc in next picot on Shawl, ch 1, sl st in top of last sc worked;

G. 4 sc in next ch-4 sp, sc in sp between ext dc dec, ch 1, sc in next picot on Shawl, ch 1, sl st in top of last sc worked;

H. 4 sc in next ch-4 sp, sc in next hdc, ch 1, sc in next picot on Shawl, ch 1, sl st in top of last sc worked;

I. 4 sc in next ch-4 sp, sc in next sc, ch 1, sc in next picot on Shawl, ch 1, sl st in top of last sc worked;

J. 4 sc in next ch-4 sp, sc in next ext dc, ch 1, sc in next picot on Shawl, ch 1, sl st in top of last sc worked;

K. 3 sc in next ch-3 sp, sc in next tr, ch 3, sl st in next ch-7 sp on point of Shawl, ch 3, sl st in top of last sc worked;

L. 3 sc in next ch-3 sp, sc in next ext dc, ch-3 picot, 4 sc in next ch-4 sp, sc in next sc, ch-3 picot;

M. 4 sc in next ch-4 sp, sc in next hdc, ch-3 picot, 4 sc in next ch-4 sp, sc in sp between ext dc dec;

N. ch-3 picot, 4 sc in next ch-4 sp, sc in next hdc, ch-3 picot, 4 sc in next ch-4 sp, sc in next sc, ch-3 picot, 4 sc in last ch-4 sp, join in beg sc. Fasten off.

5TH INNER MOTIF

Rnds 1–5: Rep rnds 1–5 of First Shamrock Motif on pages 26 and 27.

Rnd 6: Ch 1, sc in first st, ch-3 picot, 3 sc in next ch-3 sp, sc in next tr, ch 7, sl st in top of last sc worked, work following steps to complete rnd:

A. 3 sc in next ch-3 sp, sc in next ext dc, ch-3 picot, 4 sc in next ch-4 sp, sc in next sc, ch-3 picot, 4 sc in next ch-4 sp, sc in next hdc, ch-3 picot, 4 sc in next ch-4 sp, sc in sp between ext dc dec;

B. ch-3 picot, 4 sc in next ch-4 sp, sc in next hdc, ch-3 picot, 4 sc in next ch-4 sp, sc in next sc, ch-3 picot, 4 sc in next ch-4 sp, sc in next ext dc;

C. ch-3 picot, 3 sc in next ch-3 sp, sc in next tr, ch 3, sl st in same ch-7 sp on point of Shawl;

D. working up next side of Shawl, ch 3, sl st in top of last sc worked, 3 sc in next ch-3 sp, sc in next ext dc, ch 1, sc in next picot on Shawl, ch 1, sl st in top of last sc worked;

E. 4 sc in next ch-4 sp, sc in next sc, ch 1, sc in next picot on Shawl, ch 1, sl st in top of last sc worked;

F. 4 sc in next ch-4 sp, sc in next hdc, ch 1, sc in next picot on Shawl, ch 1, sl st in top of last sc worked;

G. 4 sc in next ch-4 sp, sc in sp between ext dc dec, ch 1, sc in next picot on Shawl, ch 1, sl st in top of last sc worked;

H. 4 sc in next ch-4 sp, sc in next hdc, ch 1, sc in next picot on Shawl, ch 1, sl st in top of last sc worked;

I. 4 sc in next ch-4 sp, sc in next sc, ch 1, sc in next picot on Shawl, ch 1, sl st in top of last sc worked;

J. 4 sc in next ch-4 sp, sc in next ext dc, ch 1, sc in next picot on Shawl, ch 1, sl st in top of last sc worked;

K. 3 sc in next ch-3 sp, sc in next tr, ch 3, sc in next picot on Shawl, ch 3, sl st in top of sc worked;

L. 3 sc in next ch-3 sp, sc in next ext dc, ch-3 picot, 4 sc in next ch-4 sp, sc in next sc, ch-3 picot, 4 sc in next ch-4 sp, sc in next hdc, ch-3 picot, 4 sc in next ch-4 sp, sc in sp between ext dc dec;

M. ch-3 picot, 4 sc in next ch-4 sp, sc in next hdc, ch-3 picot, 4 sc in next ch-4 sp, sc in next sc, ch-3 picot, 4 sc in last ch-4 sp, join in beg sc. Fasten off.

6TH & 7TH INNER MOTIFS
Work same as 2nd and 3rd Inner Motifs.

8TH INNER MOTIF
Rnds 1–5: Rep rnds 1–5 of First Shamrock Motif on pages 26 and 27.

Rnd 6: Ch 1, sc in first st, ch-3 picot, 3 sc in next ch-3 sp, sc in next tr, ch 7, sl st in top of last sc worked, work the following steps to complete rnd:

A. 3 sc in next ch-3 sp, sc in next ext dc, ch-3 picot, 4 sc in next ch-4 sp, sc in next sc, ch-3 picot, 4 sc in next ch-4 sp, sc in next hdc, ch-3 picot, 4 sc in next ch-4 sp, sc in sp between ext dc dec;

B. ch-3 picot, 4 sc in next ch-4 sp, sc in next hdc, ch-3 picot, 4 sc in next ch-4 sp, sc in next sc, ch-3 picot, 4 sc in next ch-4 sp, sc in next ext dc;

C. ch-3 picot, 3 sc in next ch-3 sp, sc in next tr, ch 3, sl st in same picot on Shawl as last picot Motif joining of previous Motif, ch 3, sl st in top of last sc worked, 3 sc in next ch-3 sp, sc in next ext dc;

D. ch 1, sc in next picot on Shawl, ch 1, sl st in top of last sc worked, 4 sc in next ch-4 sp, sc in next sc;

E. ch 1, sc in next picot on Shawl, ch 1, sl st in top of last sc worked, 4 sc in next ch-4 sp, sc in next hdc;

F. ch 1, sc in next picot on Shawl, ch 1, sl st in top of last sc worked, 4 sc in next ch-4 sp, sc in sp between ext dc dec;

H. ch 1, sc in next picot on Shawl, ch 1, sl st in top of last sc worked, 4 sc in next ch-4 sp, sc in next hdc;

I. ch 1, sc in next picot on Shawl, ch 1, sl st in top of last sc worked, 4 sc in next ch-4 sp, sc in next sc;

K. ch 1, sc in next picot on Shawl, ch 1, sl st in top of last sc worked, 4 sc in next ch-4 sp, sc in next ext dc;

L. ch 1, sc in next picot on Shawl, ch 1, sl st in top of last sc worked, 3 sc in next ch-3 sp, sc in next tr;

M. ch 3, sc in next ch-5 picot on Shawl, ch 3, sl st in top of sc worked, 3 sc in next ch-3 sp, sc in next ext dc;

N. ch-3 picot, 4 sc in next ch-4 sp, sc in next sc, ch-3 picot, 4 sc in next ch-4 sp, sc in next hdc, ch-3 picot, 4 sc in next ch-4 sp, sc in sp between ext dc dec;

O. ch-3 picot, 4 sc in next ch-4 sp, sc in next hdc, ch-3 picot, 4 sc in next ch-4 sp, sc in next sc, ch-3 picot, 4 sc in last ch-4 sp, join in beg sc. Fasten off.

OUTER SHAMROCK MOTIFS
FIRST OUTER MOTIF

Rnds 1–5: Rep rnds 1–5 of First Shamrock Motif on pages 26 and 27.

Rnd 6: Ch 1, sc in first st, ch-3 picot, 3 sc in next ch-3 sp, sc in next tr, ch 7, sl st in top of last sc, work the following steps to complete rnd:

A. 3 sc in next ch-3 sp, sc in next ext dc, ch-3 picot, 4 sc in next ch-4 sp, sc in next sc, ch-3 picot, 4 sc in next ch-4 sp, sc in next hdc, ch-3 picot, 4 sc in next ch-4 sp, sc in sp between ext dc dec;

B. ch-3 picot, 4 sc in next ch-4 sp, sc in next hdc, ch-3 picot, 4 sc in next ch-4 sp, sc in next sc, ch-3 picot, 4 sc in next ch-4 sp, sc in next ext dc;

C. ch-3 picot, 3 sc in next ch-3 sp, sc in next tr, ch 3, sl st in same ch-5 sp on Shawl as First Inner Motif was joined;

D. ch 3, sl st in top of last sc worked, 3 sc in next ch-3 sp, sc in next ext dc, ch 1, sl st in corresponding picot on First Inner Motif, ch 1, sl st in top of last sc worked;

E. 4 sc in next ch-4 sp, sc in next sc, ch 1, sl st in corresponding picot on First Inner Motif, ch 1, sl st in top of last sc worked;

F. 4 sc in next ch-4 sp, sc in next hdc, ch 1, sl st in corresponding picot on First Inner Motif, ch 1, sl st in top of last sc worked;

G. 4 sc in next ch-4 sp, sc in sp between ext dc dec, ch 1, sl st in corresponding picot on First Inner Motif, ch 1, sl st in top of last sc worked;

H. 4 sc in next ch-4 sp, sc in next hdc, ch 1, sl st in corresponding picot on First Inner Motif, ch 1, sl st in top of last sc worked;

I. 4 sc in next ch-4 sp, sc in next sc, ch 1, sl st in corresponding picot on First Inner Motif, ch 1, sc in top of last sc worked;

J. 4 sc in next ch-4 sp, sc in next ext dc, ch 1, sl st in corresponding picot on First Inner Motif, ch 1, sl st in top of last sc worked;

K. 3 sc in next ch-3 sp, sc in next tr, ch 3, sl st in next ch-7 sp on First Inner Motif, ch 3, sl st in top of sc worked;

L. 3 sc in next ch-3 sp, sc in next ext dc, ch-3 picot, 4 sc in next ch-4 sp, sc in next sc, ch-3 picot, 4 sc in next ch-4 sp, sc in next hdc, ch-3 picot, 4 sc in next ch-4 sp, sc in sp between ext dc dec;

M. ch-3 picot, 4 sc in next ch-4 sp, sc in next hdc, ch-3 picot, 4 sc in next ch-4 sp, sc in next sc, ch-3 picot, 4 sc in last ch-4 sp, join in beg sc. Fasten off.

2ND, 3RD & 4TH OUTER MOTIFS

Rnds 1–5: Rep rnds 1–5 of First Shamrock Motif on pages 26 and 27.

Rnd 6: Ch 1, sc in first st, ch-3 picot, 3 sc in next ch-3 sp, sc in next tr, ch 3, sl st in ch-7 sp on Inner Motif that will have you working in valley between Inner Motifs, ch 3, sl st in top of last sc, work the following steps to complete rnd:

A. 3 sc in next ch-3 sp, sc in next ext dc, ch 1, sl st in corresponding picot on Inner Motif, ch 1, sl st in top of last sc worked, 4 sc in next ch-4 sp, sc in next sc;

B. ch 1, sl st in corresponding picot on Inner Motif, ch 1, sl st in top of last sc worked, 4 sc in next ch-4 sp, sc in next hdc;

C. ch 1, sl st in corresponding picot on Inner Motif, ch 1, sl st in top of last sc worked, 4 sc in next ch-4 sp, sc in sp between ext dc dec;

D. ch 1, sl st in corresponding picot on Inner Motif, ch 1, sl st in top of last sc worked, 4 sc in next ch-4 sp, sc in next hdc;

E. ch 1, sl st in corresponding picot on Inner Motif, ch 1, sl st in top of last sc worked, 4 sc in next ch-4 sp, sc in next sc;

F. ch 1, sl st in corresponding picot on Inner Motif, ch 1, sl st in top of last sc worked, 4 sc in next ch-4 sp, sc in next ext dc;

G. ch 1, sl st in corresponding picot on Inner Motif, ch 1, sl st in top of last sc worked, 3 sc in next ch-3 sp, sc in next tr, ch 3, sl st in same worked picot on Shawl, ch-3 picot, 3 sc in next ch-3 sp, sc in next ext dc;

H. ch 1, sl st in corresponding picot on Inner Motif, ch 1, sl st in top of last sc worked, 4 sc in next ch-4 sp, sc in next sc;

I. ch 1, sl st in corresponding picot on Inner Motif, ch 1, sl st in top of last sc worked, 4 sc in next ch-4 sp, sc in next hdc;

J. ch 1, sl st in corresponding picot on Inner Motif, ch 1, sl st in top of last sc worked, 4 sc in next ch-4 sp, sc in sp between ext dc dec;

K. ch 1, sl st in corresponding picot on Inner Motif;

L. ch 1, sl st in top of last sc worked, 4 sc in next ch-4 sp, sc in next hdc;

M. ch 1, sl st in corresponding picot on Inner Motif;

N. ch 1, sl st in top of last sc worked, 4 sc in next ch-4 sp, sc in next sc;

O. ch 1, sl st in corresponding picot on Inner Motif, ch 1, sl st in top of last sc worked, 4 sc in next ch-4 sp, sc in next ext dc;

P. ch 1, sl st in corresponding picot on Inner Motif, ch 1, sl st in top of last sc worked;

Q. 3 sc in next ch-3 sp, sc in next tr, ch 3, sl st in next ch-7 sp on Inner Motif, ch 3, sl st in top of sc worked;

R. 3 sc in next ch-3 sp, sc in next ext dc, ch-3 picot, 4 sc in next ch-4 sp, sc in next sc, ch-3 picot, 4 sc in next ch-4 sp, sc in next hdc, ch-3 picot;

S. 4 sc in next ch-4 sp, sc in sp between ext dc dec, ch-3 picot, 4 sc in next ch-4 sp, sc in next hdc, ch-3 picot, 4 sc in next ch-4 sp, sc in next sc, ch-3 picot, 4 sc in last ch-4 sp, join in beg sc. Fasten off.

5TH OUTER MOTIF

Rnds 1–5: Rep rnds 1–5 of First Shamrock Motif on pages 26 and 27.

Rnd 6: Ch 1, sc in first st, ch-3 picot, 3 sc in next ch-3 sp, sc in next tr, ch 7, sl st in top of last sc worked, work the following steps to complete rnd:

A. 3 sc in next ch-3 sp, sc in next ext dc, ch-3 picot, 4 sc in next ch-4 sp, sc in next sc, ch-3 picot, 4 sc in next ch-4 sp, sc in next hdc, ch-3 picot, 4 sc in next ch-4 sp, sc in sp between ext dc dec;

B. ch-3 picot, 4 sc in next ch-4 sp, sc in next hdc, ch-3 picot, 4 sc in next ch-4 sp, sc in next sc, ch-3 picot, 4 sc in next ch-4 sp, sc in next ext dc, ch-3 picot, 3 sc in next ch-3 sp, sc in next tr, ch 3, sl st in next ch-7 sp on Inner Motif, ch 3, sl st in last sc worked;

C. 3 sc in next ch-3 sp, sc in next ext dc, ch 1, sl st in corresponding picot on Inner Motif, ch 1, sl st in top of last sc worked;

D. 4 sc in next ch-4 sp, sc in next sc, ch 1, sl st in corresponding picot on Inner Motif, ch 1, sl st in top of last sc worked;

E. 4 sc in next ch-4 sp, sc in next hdc, ch 1, sl st in corresponding picot on Inner Motif, ch 1, sl st in top of last sc worked;

F. 4 sc in next ch-4 sp, sc in sp between sts of next ext dc dec, ch 1, sl st in corresponding picot on Inner Motif, ch 1, sc in top of last sc worked;

G. 4 sc in next ch-4 sp, sc in next hdc, ch 1, sl st in corresponding picot on Inner Motif, ch 1, sl st in top of last sc worked;

H. 4 sc in next ch-4 sp, sc in next sc, ch 1, sl st in corresponding picot on First Inner Motif ch 1, sl st in top of last sc worked;

I. 4 sc in next ch-4 sp, sc in next ext dc, ch 1, sl st in corresponding picot on Inner Motif, ch 1, sl st in top of last sc worked;

J. 3 sc in next ch-3 sp, sc in next tr, ch 3, sl st in next ch-7 sp on Inner Motif, ch 3, sl st in top of sc worked;

K. 3 sc in next ch-3 sp, sc in next ext dc, ch-3 picot, 4 sc in next ch-4 sp, sc in next sc, ch-3 picot, 4 sc in next ch-4 sp, sc in next hdc, ch-3 picot, 4 sc in next ch-4 sp, sc in sp between ext dc dec;

L. ch-3 picot, 4 sc in next ch-4 sp, sc in next hdc, ch-3 picot, 4 sc in next ch-4 sp, sc in next sc, ch-3 picot, 4 sc in last ch-4 sp, join in beg sc. Fasten off.

6TH OUTER MOTIF

Rnds 1–5: Rep rnds 1–5 of First Shamrock Motif on pages 26 and 27.

Rnd 6: Ch 1, sc in first st, ch-3 picot, 3 sc in next ch-3 sp, sc in next tr, ch 7, sl st in top of last sc worked, work the following steps to complete rnd:

A. 3 sc in next ch-3 sp, sc in next ext dc, ch-3 picot, 4 sc in next ch-4 sp, sc in next sc, ch-3 picot, 4 sc in next ch-4 sp, sc in next hdc, ch-3 picot, 4 sc in next ch-4 sp, sc in sp between ext dc dec;

B. ch-3 picot, 4 sc in next ch-4 sp, sc in next hdc, ch-3 picot, 4 sc in next ch-4 sp, sc in next sc, ch-3 picot, 4 sc in next ch-4 sp, sc in next ext dc;

C. ch-3 picot, 3 sc in next ch-3 sp, sc in next tr, ch 3, sl st in same ch-7 sp at point on Shawl, ch 3, sl st in top of last sc, 3 sc in next ch-3 sp, sc in next ext dc, working on Inner Motif;

D. ch 1, sl st in corresponding picot on next Inner Motif of next side, ch 1, sl st in top of last sc worked, 4 sc in next ch-4 sp, sc in next sc;

E. ch 1, sl st in corresponding picot on Inner Motif, ch 1, sl st in top of last sc worked, 4 sc in next ch-4 sp, sc in next hdc;

F. ch 1, sl st in corresponding picot on Inner Motif, ch 1, sl st in top of last sc worked, 4 sc in next ch-4 sp, sc in sp between ext dc dec;

G. ch 1, sl st in corresponding picot on Inner Motif, ch 1, sl st in top of last sc worked, 4 sc in next ch-4 sp, sc in next hdc;

H. ch 1, sl st in corresponding picot on Inner Motif, ch 1, sl st in top of last sc worked, 4 sc in next ch-4 sp, sc in next sc;

I. ch 1, sl st in corresponding picot on Inner Motif, ch 1, sc in top of last sc worked, 4 sc in next ch-4 sp, sc in next ext dc;

J. ch 1, sl st in corresponding picot on Inner Motif, ch 1, sl st in top of last sc worked, 3 sc in next ch-3 sp, sc in next tr;

K. ch 3, sl st in next ch-7 sp on Inner Motif, ch 3, sl st in top of sc worked, 3 sc in next ch-3 sp, sc in next ext dc;

L. ch-3 picot, 4 sc in next ch-4 sp, sc in next sc, ch-3 picot, 4 sc in next ch-4 sp, sc in next hdc, ch-3 picot, 4 sc in next ch-4 sp, sc in sp between ext dc dec;

M. ch-3 picot, 4 sc in next ch-4 sp, sc in next hdc, ch-3 picot, 4 sc in next ch-4 sp, sc in next sc, ch-3 picot, 4 sc in last ch-4 sp, join in beg sc. Fasten off.

7TH OUTER MOTIF

Rnds 1–5: Rep rnds 1–5 of First Shamrock Motif on pages 26 and 27.

Rnd 6: Ch 1, sc in first st, ch-3 picot, 3 sc in next ch-3 sp, sc in next tr, ch 3, sl st in ch-7 sp on Outer Motif that will have you working in valley between Outer Motifs, this is worked between 5th and 6th Outer Motifs, ch 3, sl st in top of last sc worked, work the following steps to complete rnd:

A. 3 sc in next ch-3 sp, sc in next ext dc, ch 1, sl st in corresponding picot on Outer Motif, ch 1, sl st in top of last sc worked, 4 sc in next ch-4 sp, sc in next sc;

B. ch 1, sl st in corresponding picot on Outer Motif, ch 1, sl st in top of last sc worked, 4 sc in next ch-4 sp, sc in next hdc;

C. ch 1, sl st in corresponding picot on Outer Motif, ch 1, sl st in top of last sc worked, 4 sc in next ch-4 sp, sc in sp between ext dc dec;

D. ch 1, sl st in corresponding picot on Outer Motif, ch 1, sl st in top of last sc worked, 4 sc in next ch-4 sp, sc in next hdc;

E. ch 1, sl st in corresponding picot on Outer Motif, ch 1, sl st in top of last sc worked, 4 sc in next ch-4 sp, sc in next sc;

F. ch 1, sl st in corresponding picot on Outer Motif, ch 1, sl st in top of last sc worked, 4 sc in next ch-4 sp, sc in next ext dc;

G. ch 1, sl st in corresponding picot on Outer Motif, ch 1, sl st in top of last sc worked, 3 sc in next ch-3 sp, sc in next tr;

H. ch 3, sl st in same ch-7 at point on Shawl, ch 3, sl st in top of last sc worked, 3 sc in next ch-3 sp, sc in next ext dc;

I. working on 6th Motif of Outer Shamrock Motif, ch 1, sl st in corresponding picot on Outer Motif, ch 1, sl st in top of last sc worked, 4 sc in next ch-4 sp, sc in next sc;

J. ch 1, sl st in corresponding picot on Outer Motif, ch 1, sl st in top of last sc worked, 4 sc in next ch-4 sp, sc in next hdc;

K. ch 1, sl st in corresponding picot on Outer Motif, ch 1, sl st in top of last sc worked, 4 sc in next ch-4 sp, sc in sp between ext dc dec;

L. ch 1, sl st in corresponding picot on Outer Motif, ch 1, sl st in top of last sc worked, 4 sc in next ch-4 sp, sc in next hdc;

M. ch 1, sl st in corresponding picot on Outer Motif, ch 1, sl st in top of last sc worked, 4 sc in next ch-4 sp, sc in next sc;

N. ch 1, sl st in corresponding picot on Outer Motif, ch 1, sc in top of last sc worked, 4 sc in next ch-4 sp, sc in next ext dc;

O. ch 1, sl st in corresponding picot on Outer Motif, ch 1, sl st in top of last sc worked, 3 sc in next ch-3 sp, sc in next tr;

P. ch 3, sl st in next ch-7 sp on Outer Motif, ch 3, sl st in top of sc worked, 3 sc in next ch-3 sp, sc in next ext dc;

Q. ch-3 picot, 4 sc in next ch-4 sp, sc in next sc, ch-3 picot, 4 sc in next ch-4 sp, sc in next hdc, ch-3 picot, 4 sc in next ch-4 sp, sc in sp between ext dc dec;

R. ch-3 picot, 4 sc in next ch-4 sp, sc in next hdc, ch-3 picot, 4 sc in next ch-4 sp, sc in next sc, ch-3 picot, 4 sc in last ch-4 sp, join in beg sc. Fasten off.

8TH OUTER MOTIF

Rnds 1–5: Rep rnds 1–5 of First Shamrock Motif on pages 26 and 27.

Rnd 6: Ch 1, sc in first st, ch-3 picot, 3 sc in next ch-3 sp, sc in next tr, ch 7, sl st in top of last sc, work the following steps to complete rnd:

A. 3 sc in next ch-3 sp, sc in next ext dc, ch-3 picot, 4 sc in next ch-4 sp, sc in next sc, ch-3 picot, 4 sc in next ch-4 sp, sc in next hdc, ch-3 picot, 4 sc in next ch-4 sp, sc in sp between ext dc dec;

B. ch-3 picot, 4 sc in next ch-4 sp, sc in next hdc, ch-3 picot, 4 sc in next ch-4 sp, sc in next sc, ch-3 picot, 4 sc in next ch-4 sp, sc in next ext dc;

C. ch-3 picot, 3 sc in next ch-3 sp, sc in next tr, working on bottom edge of 7th Outer Motif, ch 3, sl st in same ch-7 sp on bottom edge of 7th Outer Motif, ch 3, sl st in top of last sc worked;

D. 3 sc in next ch-3 sp, sc in next ext dc, ch 1, sl st in corresponding picot on 7th Outer Motif, ch 1, sl st in top of last sc worked;

E. 4 sc in next ch-4 sp, sc in next sc, ch 1, sl st in corresponding picot on 7th Outer Motif, ch 1, sl st in top of last sc worked;

F. 4 sc in next ch-4 sp, sc in next hdc, sl st in corresponding picot on 7th Outer Motif, ch 1, sl st in top of last sc worked;

G. 4 sc in next ch-4 sp, sc in sp between ext dc dec, ch 1, sl st in corresponding picot on 7th Outer Motif, ch 1, sl st in top of last sc worked;

H. 4 sc in next ch-4 sp, sc in next hdc, ch 1, sl st in corresponding picot on 7th Outer Motif, ch 1, sl st in top of last sc worked;

I. 4 sc in next ch-4 sp, sc in next sc, ch 1, sl st in corresponding picot on 7th Outer Motif, ch 1, sc in top of last sc worked;

J. 4 sc in next ch-4 sp, sc in next ext dc, ch 1, sl st in corresponding picot on 7th Outer Motif, ch 1, sl st in top of last sc worked;

K. 3 sc in next ch-3 sp, sc in next tr, ch 3, sl st in next ch-7 sp on 7th Outer Motif, ch 3, sl st in top of sc worked;

L. 3 sc in next ch-3 sp, sc in next ext dc, ch-3 picot, 4 sc in next ch-4 sp, sc in next sc, ch-3 picot, 4 sc in next ch-4 sp, sc in next hdc, ch-3 picot, 4 sc in next ch-4 sp, sc in sp between ext dc dec;

M. ch-3 picot, 4 sc in next ch-4 sp, sc in next hdc, ch-3 picot, 4 sc in next ch-4 sp, sc in next sc, ch-3 picot, 4 sc in last ch-4 sp, join in beg sc. Fasten off.

9TH–11TH OUTER MOTIFS

Rnds 1–5: Rep rnds 1–5 of First Shamrock Motif on pages 26 and 27.

Rnd 6: Ch 1, sc in first st, ch-3 picot, 3 sc in next ch-3 sp, sc in next tr, ch 3, sl st in ch-7 sp on Inner Motif that will have you working in valley between Inner Motifs on next side of Shawl, ch 3, sl st in top of last sc, work the following steps to complete rnd:

A. 3 sc in next ch-3 sp, sc in next ext dc, ch 1, sl st in corresponding picot on Inner Motif, ch 1, sl st in top of last sc worked, 4 sc in next ch-4 sp, sc in next sc;

B. ch 1, sl st in corresponding picot on Inner Motif, ch 1, sl st in top of last sc worked, 4 sc in next ch-4 sp, sc in next hdc;

C. ch 1, sl st in corresponding picot on Inner Motif, ch 1, sl st in top of last sc worked, 4 sc in next ch-4 sp, sc in sp between ext dc dec;

D. ch 1, sl st in corresponding picot on Inner Motif, ch 1, sl st in top of last sc worked, 4 sc in next ch-4 sp, sc in next hdc;

E. ch 1, sl st in corresponding picot on Inner Motif, ch 1, sl st in top of last sc worked, 4 sc in next ch-4 sp, sc in next sc;

F. ch 1, sl st in corresponding picot on Inner Motif, ch 1, sl st in top of last sc worked, 4 sc in next ch-4 sp, sc in next ext dc, ch 1, sl st in corresponding picot on Inner Motif;

G. ch 1, sl st in top of last sc worked, 3 sc in next ch-3 sp, sc in next tr, ch 3, sl st in same picot on Shawl, ch-3 picot, 3 sc in next ch-3 sp, sc in next ext dc;

H. ch 1, sl st in corresponding picot on Inner Motif, ch 1, sl st in top of last sc worked, 4 sc in next ch-4 sp, sc in next sc;

I. ch 1, sl st in corresponding picot on Inner Motif, ch 1, sl st in top of last sc worked, 4 sc in next ch-4 sp, sc in next hdc;

J. ch 1, sl st in corresponding picot on Inner Motif, ch 1, sl st in top of last sc worked, 4 sc in next ch-4 sp, sc in sp between ext dc dec;

K. ch 1, sl st in corresponding picot on Inner Motif, ch 1, sl st in top of last sc worked, 4 sc in next ch-4 sp, sc in next hdc;

L. ch 1, sl st in corresponding picot on Inner Motif, ch 1, sl st in top of last sc worked, 4 sc in next ch-4 sp, sc in next sc;

M. ch 1, sl st in corresponding picot on Inner Motif, ch 1, sc in top of last sc worked, 4 sc in next ch-4 sp, sc in next ext dc;

N. ch 1, sl st in corresponding picot on Inner Motif, ch 1, sl st in top of last sc worked, 3 sc in next ch-3 sp, sc in next tr;

O. ch 3, sl st in next ch-7 sp on Inner Motif, ch 3, sl st in top of sc worked, 3 sc in next ch-3 sp, sc in next ext dc;

P. ch-3 picot, 4 sc in next ch-4 sp, sc in next sc, ch-3 picot, 4 sc in next ch-4 sp, sc in next hdc;

Q. ch-3 picot, 4 sc in next ch-4 sp, sc in sp between ext dc dec, ch-3 picot, 4 sc in next ch-4 sp, sc in next hdc;

R. ch-3 picot, 4 sc in next ch-4 sp, sc in next sc, ch-3 picot, 4 sc in last ch-4 sp, join in beg sc. Fasten off.

12TH OUTER MOTIF

Rnds 1–5: Rep rnds 1–5 of First Shamrock Motif on pages 26 and 27.

Rnd 6: Ch 1, sc in first st, ch-3 picot, 3 sc in next ch-3 sp, sc in next tr, ch 7, sl st in top of last sc worked, work the following steps to complete rnd:

A. 3 sc in next ch-3 sp, sc in next ext dc, ch-3 picot, 4 sc in next ch-4 sp, sc in next sc, ch-3 picot, 4 sc in next ch-4 sp, sc in next hdc, ch-3 picot, 4 sc in next ch-4 sp, sc in sp between ext dc dec;

B. ch-3 picot, 4 sc in next ch-4 sp, sc in next hdc, ch-3 picot, 4 sc in next ch-4 sp, sc in next sc, ch-3 picot, 4 sc in next ch-4 sp, sc in next ext dc, ch-3 picot, 3 sc in next ch-3 sp, sc in next tr, ch 3, sl st in ch-7 sp on last Inner Motif, ch 3, sl st in top of last sc worked, 3 sc in next ch-3 sp, sc in next ext dc;

C. ch 1, sl st in corresponding picot on Inner Motif, ch 1, sl st in top of last sc worked, 4 sc in next ch-4 sp, sc in next sc;

D. ch 1, sl st in corresponding picot on Inner Motif, ch 1, sl st in top of last sc worked, 4 sc in next ch-4 sp, sc in next hdc;

E. ch 1, sl st in corresponding picot on Inner Motif, ch 1, sl st in top of last sc worked, 4 sc in next ch-4 sp, sc in sp between ext dc dec;

F. ch 1, sl st in corresponding picot on Inner Motif, ch 1, sl st in top of last sc worked, 4 sc in next ch-4 sp, sc in next hdc;

G. ch 1, sl st in corresponding picot on Inner Motif, ch 1, sl st in top of last sc worked, 4 sc in next ch-4 sp, sc in next sc;

H. ch 1, sl st in corresponding picot on Inner Motif, ch 1, sc in top of last sc worked, 4 sc in next ch-4 sp, sc in next ext dc;

I. ch 1, sl st in corresponding picot on Shawl, ch 1, sl st in top of last sc worked, 3 sc in next ch-3 sp, sc in next tr;

J. ch 3, sl st in same ch-5 sp on Inner Motif, ch 3, sl st in top of sc worked, 3 sc in next ch-3 sp, sc in next ext dc;

K. ch-3 picot, 4 sc in next ch-4 sp, sc in next sc, ch-3 picot, 4 sc in next ch-4 sp, sc in next hdc, ch-3 picot, 4 sc in next ch-4 sp, sc in sp between next ext dc dec;

L. ch-3 picot, 4 sc in next ch-4 sp, sc in next hdc, ch-3 picot, 4 sc in next ch-4 sp, sc in next sc, ch-3 picot, 4 sc in last ch-4 sp, join in beg sc. Fasten off.

3RD PICOT ROWS

Row 1: With WS facing, join in ch-7 sp on upper edge of Shawl that will have you working toward the point of Shawl, ch 6, (dc, ch 4, dc) in same ch sp, *[ch 4, dc in next picot] 7 times, ch 4, dc in base of ch-7 sp on same Motif, ch 4, dc in ch-7 sp on Inner Motif, ch 4, dc in base of ch-7 sp on next Outer Motif, rep from * 4 times, [ch 4, dc in next picot] 7 times, ch 4, (tr, {ch 2, tr} 5 times) in next ch-7 sp on point of Shawl, **[ch 4, dc in next picot] 7 times, ch 4, dc in base of ch-7 sp on same Motif, ch 4, dc in ch-7 sp on Inner Motif, ch 4, dc in base of ch-7 sp on next Outer Motif, rep from ** 4 times, [ch 4, dc in next picot] 7 times, ch 4, (dc, ch 4, dc, ch 3, dc) in next ch-7 sp on last Outer Motif, turn.

Row 2: Ch 1, 3 sc in first ch-3 sp, 5 sc in each of next 59 ch-4 sps, 3 sc in each of next 5 ch-2 sps, 5 sc in each of next 59 ch-4 sps, 3 sc in last ch-3 sp, turn.

Row 3: Ch 1, sc in first st, [ch-5 picot ch, sk next 4 sts, sc in next sc] 61 times, ch-5 picot ch, sk next sc, sc in next sc, [ch-5 picot ch, sk next 4 sts, sc in next st] 61 times, turn.

Rows 4 & 5: Ch 1, sc in first st, ch 9, sl st in 4th ch from hook, ch 2, sc in ch sp between picots, [ch-5 picot ch, sc between next 2 picots] 61 times, ch-5 picot ch, sc in same ch sp, [ch-5 picot ch, sc in ch sp between picots] 61 times, ch 5, sl st in 4th ch from hook, ch 2, dtr in last st, forming last ch sp, turn.

Row 6: Ch 1, sc in last ch sp, ch 9, sc in ch sp between next 2 picots, ch 6, sc in ch sp between next 2 picots, ch 6, sl st in 4th ch from hook, ch 3, sc in ch sp between next 2 picots, *[ch 6, sc in ch sp between next 2 picots] twice, ch 6, sl st in 4th ch from hook, ch 3, sc in ch sp between next 2 picots, rep from * 18 times, [ch 6, sc in ch sp between next 2 picots] twice, ch 7, sc in same ch sp, **[ch 6, sc in ch sp between next 2 picots] twice, ch 6, sl st in 4th ch from hook, ch 3, sc in ch sp between next 2 petals, rep from ** 19 times, ch 6, sc in ch sp between next 2 picots, ch 9, sc in last st. Fasten off.

2ND ROW OF ROSES
FIRST ROSE
Rnds 1–4: Rep rnds 1–4 of First Rose on First Row of Roses on page 29.

Rnd 5: Ch 1, (sc, 7 dc, sc) in first ch sp and in each of next 3 ch sps, (sc, 4 dc) in next ch sp, sl st in next ch-9 sp of beg of row 6 of 3rd Picot Rows, making sure Rose faces RS of Shawl, (3 dc, sc) in same ch sp on this Rose, (sc, 4 dc) in next ch sp, sl st in next ch-6 sp on row 6 of 3rd Picot Rows, (sc, 3 dc) in same ch sp on this Rose, join in beg sc. Fasten off.

2ND–21ST ROSES
Rnds 1–4: Rep rnds 1–4 of First Rose on First Row of Roses on page 29.

Rnd 5: Ch 1, (sc, 7 dc, sc) in first ch sp and in each of next 2 ch sps, (sc, dc) in next ch sp, sl st in 4th dc of petal on last Rose closest to Shawl that will have you working toward Shawl, (3 dc, sc) in same ch sp on this Rose, (sc, 4 dc) in next ch sp, sk next ch sp with picot on Shawl, sl st in next ch-6 sp, (3 dc, sc) in same ch sp on this Rose, (sc, 4 dc) in next ch sp, sl st in next ch-6 sp on Shawl, (3 dc, sc) in same ch sp on this Rose, join in beg sc. Fasten off.

22ND ROSE
Rnds 1–4: Rep rnds 1–4 of First Rose on First Row of Roses on page 29.

Rnd 5: Ch 1, (sc, 7 dc, sc) in first ch sp and in each of next 3 ch sps, (sc, 4 dc) in next ch sp, sl st in 4th dc of petal on last Rose, (3 dc, sc) in same ch sp on this Rose, (sc, 4 dc) in next ch sp, sl st in next ch-7 sp on point of Shawl, (sc, 3 dc) in same ch sp on this Rose, join in beg sc. Fasten off.

23RD ROSE
Rnds 1–4: Rep rnds 1–4 of First Rose on First Row of Roses on page 29.

Rnd 5: Ch 1, (sc, 7 dc, sc) in first ch sp and in each of next 2 ch sps, (sc, 4 dc) in next ch sp, sl st in 4th dc of petal on last Rose, (3 dc, sc) in same ch sp on this Rose, (sc, 4 dc) in next ch sp, sl st in next ch-6 sp on Shawl, (sc, 3 dc) in same ch sp on this Rose, (sc, 4 dc) in next ch sp, sl st in next ch-6 sp on Shawl, (3 dc, sc) in same ch sp on this Rose, join in beg sc. Fasten off.

24TH–42ND ROSES
Rnds 1–4: Rep rnds 1–4 of First Rose on First Row of Roses on page 29.

Rnd 5: Ch 1, (sc, 7 dc, sc) in first ch sp and in each of next 2 ch sps, (sc, dc) in next ch sp, sl st in 4th dc of petal on last Rose closest to Shawl that will have you working toward Shawl, (3 dc, sc) in same ch sp on this Rose, (sc, 4 dc) in next ch sp, sk next ch sp with picot on Shawl, sl st in next ch-6 sp, (3 dc, sc) in same ch sp on this Rose, (sc, 4 dc) in next ch sp, sl st in next ch-6 sp on Shawl, (3 dc, sc) in same ch sp on this Rose, join in beg sc. Fasten off.

LAST ROSE

Rnds 1–4: Rep rnds 1–4 of First Rose on First Row of Roses on page 29.

Rnd 5: Ch 1, (sc, 7 dc, sc) in first ch sp and in each of next 2 ch sps, (sc, dc) in next ch sp, sl st in 4th dc of petal on last Rose closest to Shawl that will have you working toward Shawl, (3 dc, sc) in same ch sp on this Rose, (sc, 4 dc) in next ch sp, sk next ch sp with picot on Shawl, sl st in next ch-6 sp, (3 dc, sc) in same ch sp on this Rose, (sc, 4 dc) in next ch sp, sl st in next ch-9 sp on Shawl, (3 dc, sc) in same ch sp on this Rose, join in beg sc. Fasten off.

4TH PICOT ROWS

Row 1: With RS facing, join in 4th dc of first free petal of Rose at end of row that will have you working toward the next free petal on same Rose, ch 9, sc in 4th dc of next petal, ch 5, sc in next 4th dc of next petal, [ch 6, sc in 4th dc of next petal on next Rose, ch 5, sc in 4th dc of next petal on same Rose] 20 times, ch 6, dc in 4th dc of next petal on center Rose on point, ch 5, (tr, ch 5, dtr, ch 5, tr) in 4th dc on next petal, ch 5, dc in 4th dc of next petal, [ch 6, sc in 4th dc of next petal on next Rose, ch 5, sc in 4th dc of next petal on same Rose] 21 times, ch 4, dtr in next petal on last Rose, forming last ch sp, turn.

Row 2: Ch 1, sc in last ch sp, (ch-5 picot ch, sc) twice in same ch sp, [ch-5 picot ch, sc in next ch-5 sp, ch-5 picot ch, sc in next ch-6 sp, ch-5 picot ch, sc in same ch sp] 21 times, [ch-5 picot ch, sc in next ch-5 sp] twice, ch-5 picot ch, sc in same ch sp, ch-5 picot ch, sc in next ch-5 sp, ch-5 picot ch, sc in same ch sp, [ch-5 picot ch, sc in next ch-5 sp, ch-5 picot ch, sc in next ch-6 sp, ch-5 picot ch, sc in same ch sp] 21 times, ch-5 picot ch, sc in next ch-5 sp, ch-5 picot ch, sc in next ch-9 sp, [ch-5 picot ch, sc in same ch sp] twice, turn.

Rows 3–5: Ch 1, sc in first st, ch 9, sl st in 4th ch from hook, ch 2, sc in ch sp between next 2 picots, [ch-5 picot ch, sc in ch sp between next 2 picots] 68 times, ch-5 picot ch, sc in same ch sp, [ch-5 picot ch, sc in ch sp between next 2 picots] 68 times, ch 5, sl st in 4th ch from hook, ch 2, dtr in last sc, forming last ch sp, turn.

EDGING

Rnd 1: Ch 1, sc in last ch sp, ch 6 sc in same ch sp, [ch 6, sc in ch sp between next 2 picots] 69 times, ch 6, sc in same ch sp, [ch 6, sc in ch sp between next 2 picots] 69 times, ch 6, sc in same ch sp, working in ends of rows across top edge of Shawl, evenly sp (ch 5, sc) 72 times across, join in beg sc.

Row 2: Now working in rows, ch 1, sc in first st, (3 sc, ch 3, 3 sc) in each of next 141 ch-6 sps, leaving rem sts unworked, turn.

Rnd 3: Now working in rnds, sl st in each of next 3 sts, sl st in next ch sp, ch 2, (4 dc, ch 3, 3 dc) in same ch sp, (ch 3, 3 dc, ch 3, 3 dc) in each of next 69 ch-3 sps, ch 3, (3 dc, {ch 3, 3 dc} 3 times) in ch-6 sp at point of Shawl, (ch 3, 3 dc, ch 3, 3 dc) in each of next 69 ch-3 sps, ch 3, (3 dc, ch 3, 5 dc) in next ch-3 sp, working across top edge of Shawl, (3 dc, ch-3 picot, 2 dc) in each ch-5 sp across, join in 2nd ch of beg ch-2.

Row 4: Now working in rows, sl st in each st across to first ch-3 sp, sl st in ch sp, ch 4, (tr, {ch 3, 2 tr} 3 times) in same ch sp, ch 3, (2 tr, {ch 3, 2 tr} 3 times, ch 3) in each of next 70 ch-3 sps, (2 tr, {ch 3, 2 tr} 5 times) in next ch-3 sp, ch 3, (2 tr, {ch 3, 2 tr} 3 times, ch 3) in each of next 70 ch-3 sps, (2 tr, {ch 3, 2 tr} 3 times) in ch-3 sp, leaving rem sts unworked, turn.

Row 5: Ch 1, sc in first st, *[ch-5 picot ch, sc in next ch-3 sp] down side until you sc in center ch-3 sp on point of Shawl, ch-5 picot ch, sc in same ch sp, [ch-5 picot ch, sc in next ch-3 sp] up side until you sc in last ch-3 sp at end of Shawl, sl st in each of next 2 tr, leaving rem sts unworked, turn.

Row 6: Ch 1, sc in first st, ch 9, sl st in 4th ch from hook, sc in ch sp between next 2 picots, [ch-5 picot ch, sc in ch sp between next 2 picots] down side until you sc between 2 picots on center ch sp on point of Shawl, ch-5 picot ch, sc in same ch sp, [ch-5 picot ch, sc in ch sp between next 2 picots] up side until you sc between 2 picots on next to last ch-5 picot ch, ch 5 sl st in 4th ch from hook, ch 2, dtr in last st, forming last ch sp, turn.

Row 7: Ch 1, sc in last ch sp, [ch 6, sc in ch sp between next 2 picots] down side until you sc between 2 picots on center ch at point of Shawl, ch 9, sc in same ch sp, [ch 6, sc in next ch sp between next 2 picots] up side until you sc between last 2 picots, turn.

Row 8: Ch 1, (2 sc, {ch 3, 2 sc} 3 times) in first ch-6 sp and in each ch-6 sp down side to ch-9 sp, (2 sc, {ch 3, 2 sc} 5 times) in ch-9 sp, (2 sc, {ch 3, 2 sc} 3 times) in each ch-6 sp across. Fasten off.

Block. ■

Irish Whisper Doily

SKILL LEVEL

INTERMEDIATE

FINISHED SIZE
15 inches across

MATERIALS
- Size 10 crochet cotton:
  250 yds white
- Size 7/1.65mm steel crochet hook or size needed to obtain gauge

GAUGE
Rnds 1–3 = 2 inches across

PATTERN NOTES
Join with slip stitch as indicated unless otherwise stated.

Chain-2 at beginning of row or round counts as first double crochet unless otherwise stated.

Chain-3 at beginning of row or round counts as first treble crochet unless otherwise stated.

Weave in loose ends as work progresses.

SPECIAL STITCHES
Triple picot: Ch 4, sl st in front lp and front strand of last st worked, ch 5, sl st in same st catching front lp of first ch of beg ch-4, ch 4, sl st in same st catching front lp of beg ch-4 and ch-5.

Chain-3 picot (ch-3 picot): Ch 3, sl st in top of last st worked.

Double treble crochet decrease (dtr dec): Holding last lp of each st on hook, dtr in next sc, sk next 6 sc, dtr in next sc, yo, pull through all lps on hook.

Cluster (cl): Holding back last lp of each st on hook, 4 tr as indicated in instructions.

INSTRUCTIONS
DOILY

Rnd 1: Ch 5, sl st in first ch to form ring, **ch 2** *(see Pattern Notes)*, 15 dc in ring, **join** *(see Pattern Notes)* in 2nd ch of beg ch-2. *(16 dc)*

Rnd 2: Ch 2, **fpdc** *(see Stitch Guide)* around same st, [dc in next dc, fpdc around same dc] around, join in 2nd ch of beg ch-2.

Rnd 3: Ch 1, sc in each of first 3 sts, **fpsc** *(see Stitch Guide)* around next fpdc, work the following steps to complete rnd:

A. Ch 9, sl st in 9th ch from hook to form ring, ch 1, (sc, hdc, 3 dc, **ch-3 picot**—*see Special Stitches*, {4 dc, ch-3 picot} twice, 2 dc, hdc, sc) in ch-9 sp, sc around base of ch-9 ring *(medallion complete)*;

B. *sc in each of next 3 sts, fpsc around next fpdc, ch 9, sl st in 9th ch from hook to form ring, ch 1, (sc, hdc, 3 dc) in ring, ch 1, sl st in last ch-3 picot on previous medallion;

C. ch 1, sl st in top of last dc, (4 dc, ch-3 picot) 2 times in same ring, (2 dc, hdc, sc) in same ring, sc around base of ch-9 ring;

D. rep from * in step B 5 times, sc in each of next 3 sts, fpsc around next fpdc;

E. ch 9, sl st in 9th ch from hook to form ring, ch 1, (sc, hdc, 3 dc) in ring, ch 1, sl st in last ch-3 picot on previous medallion, ch 1, sl st in top of last dc, (4 dc, ch-3 picot, 4 dc) in same ring;

F. ch 1, sl st in first picot on first medallion at beg of rnd, ch 1, sl st in top of last dc, (2 dc, hdc, sc) in same ring, sc around base of ch-9 ring, join in beg sc. Fasten off.

Rnd 4: Join in any free ch-3 picot on any medallion, ch 1, sc in same st, ch 10, [sc in next ch-3 picot on next medallion, ch 10] around, join in first sc.

Rnd 5: Ch 1, sc in first st, 11 sc in next ch-10 sp, [sc in next st, 11 sc in next ch-10 sp] around, join in beg sc.

Rnd 6: Ch 1, sc in first st, ch 3, [sc in each of next 3 sts, ch 3] around, ending with sc in each of last 2 sts, join in beg sc.

Rnd 7: Sl st to center of first ch-3 sp, ch 1, sc in same ch sp, [ch 5, sl st in 4th ch from hook] twice, ch 2, *sc in next ch-3 sp, [ch 5, sl st in 4th ch from hook] twice, ch 2, rep from * around, join in beg sc.

Rnd 8: Sl st up to and in ch sp between next 2 picots, ch 1, sc in same ch sp, ch 6, sl st in 4th ch from hook, ch 5, sl st in 4th ch from hook, ch 3, *sc in ch sp between next 2 picots, ch 6, sl st in 4th ch from hook, ch 5, sl st in 4th ch from hook, ch 3, rep from * around, join in beg sc.

Rnd 9: Sl st up to and in ch sp between next 2 picots, ch 1, sc in same ch sp, *ch 7, sl st in 4th ch from hook, ch 5, sl st in 4th ch from hook, ch 4**, sc in ch sp between next 2 picots, rep from * around, ending last rep at **, join in beg sc.

Rnd 10: Sl st up to and in ch sp between next 2 picots, **ch 3** *(see Pattern Notes)*, 2 tr in same ch sp, ch 6, [3 tr in next ch sp between next 2 picots, ch 6] around, join in 3rd ch of beg ch-3.

Rnd 11: Ch 2, fpdc around next tr, dc in next tr, ch 2, 3 dc in next ch-6 sp, ch 2, [dc in next tr, fpdc around next tr, dc in next tr, ch 2, 3 dc in next ch-6 sp, ch 2] around, ending with sl st in 2nd ch of beg ch-2.

Rnd 12: Ch 1, sc in first st, fpsc around next fpdc, ch 9, sl st in 9th ch from hook to form ring, ch 1, (sc, hdc, 3 dc, ch 5, sl st in top of last dc, 4 dc, ch-3 picot, 4 dc, ch-5 sl st in top of last dc, 2 dc, hdc, sc) in ch-9 sp, sc around base of ch-9 ring, work following steps to complete rnd:

A. Sc in next dc, 2 sc in next ch-2 sp, sc in each of next 2 sts, ch-3 picot, sc in next dc, 2 sc in next ch-2 sp;

B. *sc in next dc, fpsc around next fpdc, ch 9, sl st in 9th ch from hook to form ring, ch 1, (sc, hdc, 3 dc, ch 2, sl st in last ch-5 sp on previous medallion, ch 2, sl st in top of last dc, 4 dc, ch-3 picot, 4 dc, ch-5 sl st in top of last dc, 2 dc, hdc, sc) in ch-9 sp, sc around base of ch-9 ring, sc in next dc, 2 sc in next ch-2 sp, sc in each of next 2 sts, ch-3 picot, sc in next dc, 2 sc in next ch-2 sp, rep from * 21 times;

C. sc in next st, fpsc around next fpdc, ch 9, sl st in 9th ch from hook to form ring, ch 1, (sc, hdc, 3 dc, ch 2, sl st in last ch 5 sp on previous medallion, ch 2, sl st in top of last dc, 4 dc, ch-3 picot, 4 dc, ch 2, sl st in next ch-5 sp on first medallion, ch 2, sl st in top of last dc, 2 dc, hdc, sc) in ch-9 sp, sc around base of ch-9 ring;

D. sc in next dc, 2 sc in next ch-2 sp, sc in each of next 2 sts, ch-3 picot, sc in next dc, 2 sc in next ch-2 sp, join in beg sc. Fasten off.

Rnd 13: Join in any free ch-3 picot on any medallion, ch 1, sc in same picot, ch 11, [sc in picot on next medallion, ch 11] around, join in beg sc.

Rnd 14: Ch 2, 11 dc in next ch-11 sp, [dc in next sc, 11 dc in next ch-11 sp] around, join in 2nd ch of beg ch-2.

Rnd 15: Ch 1, sc in each of first 12 sts, ch 5, turn:

A. Sk next 5 sc, (tr, ch 4, tr) in next st, ch 5, sk next 4 sts, sc in next sc, sl st in next dc, turn;

B. ch 1, (4 sc, ch-3 picot, 3 sc) in first ch-5 sp, 5 sc in next ch-4 sp, 7 sc in next ch-5 sp, sc in each of next 12 dc on this rnd, ch 5, turn;

C. sk next 5 sc, (tr, ch 4, tr) in next sc, ch 5, sk next 4 sc, sc in next sc, sl st in next sc, turn;

D. ch 1, 7 sc in first ch-5 sp, 2 sc in next ch-4 sp, ch 6, turn;

E. sk next 3 sc above next ch-5 sp, **dtr dec** (see Special Stitches), ch 6, sc in 2nd sc above next ch-4 sp, sl st in next sc, turn;

F. ch 1, (5 sc, ch-3 picot, 4 sc) in next ch-6 sp, sc in sp between sts on next dtr dec, ch-3 picot, 2 sc in next ch-6 sp, ch 8, turn;

G. sk next 3 sc, sc in next sc, turn;

H. ch 1, (sc, 2 hdc, 3 dc, ch-3 picot, 4 dc, **triple picot**—see Special Stitches, 4 dc, ch-3 picot, 2 dc, 2 hdc, sc) in first ch-8 sp;

I. (3 sc, ch-3 picot, 3 sc) in next same worked ch-6 sp, 3 sc in next same worked ch-4 sp, (4 sc, ch-3 picot, 3 sc) in next ch-6 sp, *sc in each of next 12 dc on this rnd, ch 5, turn;

J. sk next 5 sc, (tr, ch 4, tr) in next sc, ch 5, sk next 4 sc, sc in next sc, sl st in next sc, turn;

K. ch 1, (4 sc, ch-3 picot, 3 sc) in next ch-5 sp, 5 sc in next ch-4 sp, 7 sc in next ch-5 sp, sc in each of next 12 dc on this rnd, ch 5, turn;

L. sk next 5 sc, (tr, ch 4, tr) in next sc, ch 5, sk next 4 sc, sc in next sc, sl st in next sc, turn;

M. ch 1, 7 sc in next ch-5 sp, 2 sc in next ch-4 sp, ch 6, turn;

N. sk next 3 sc above next ch-5 sp, dtr dec, ch 6, sc in 2nd sc of next ch-4 sp, sl st in next sc, turn;

O. ch 1, (5 sc, ch-3 picot, 4 sc) in next ch-6 sp, sc in sp between 2 dtr sts on next dtr dec, ch-3 picot, 2 sc in next ch-6 sp, ch 8, turn;

P. sk next 3 sc, sc in next sc, turn;

Q. ch 1, (sc, 2 hdc, 3 dc, ch-3 picot, 4 dc, triple picot, 4 dc, ch-3 picot, 2 dc, 2 hdc, sc) in next ch-8 sp, (3 sc, ch-3 picot, 3 sc) in next same worked ch-6 sp, 3 sc in next same worked ch-4 sp, (4 sc, ch-3 picot, sc) in next ch-6 sp, rep from * in step I around, join in beg sc. Fasten off.

Rnd 16: Join in first ch-3 picot on point that will have you working toward the triple picot, *[ch 7, sl st in 4th ch from hook, ch 4, sc in next ch-3 picot] twice, ch 5, sl st in 4th ch from hook, ch 2, sc in first ch-4 sp on triple picot, ch 5, sl st in 4th ch from hook, ch 2, **cl** (see Special Stitches) in ch-5 sp on triple picot, triple picot in cl just worked, ch 5, sl st in 4th ch from hook, ch 2, sc in next ch-4 sp of triple picot, ch 5, sl st in 4th ch from hook, ch 2, sc in next ch-3 picot, [ch 7, sl st in 4th ch from hook, ch 3, sc in next ch-3 picot] twice, ch 5, sl st in 4th ch from hook, ch 2**, sc in next ch-3 picot, rep from * around, ending last rep at **, join in beg sc. Fasten off.

Block. ■

STITCH GUIDE

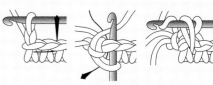

STITCH ABBREVIATIONS

beg	begin/begins/beginning
bpdc	back post double crochet
bpsc	back post single crochet
bptr	back post treble crochet
CC	contrasting color
ch(s)	chain(s)
ch-	refers to chain or space previously made (i.e., ch-1 space)
ch sp(s)	chain space(s)
cl(s)	cluster(s)
cm	centimeter(s)
dc	double crochet (singular/plural)
dc dec	double crochet 2 or more stitches together, as indicated
dec	decrease/decreases/decreasing
dtr	double treble crochet
ext	extended
fpdc	front post double crochet
fpsc	front post single crochet
fptr	front post treble crochet
g	gram(s)
hdc	half double crochet
hdc dec	half double crochet 2 or more stitches together, as indicated
inc	increase/increases/increasing
lp(s)	loop(s)
MC	main color
mm	millimeter(s)
oz	ounce(s)
pc	popcorn(s)
rem	remain/remains/remaining
rep(s)	repeat(s)
rnd(s)	round(s)
RS	right side
sc	single crochet (singular/plural)
sc dec	single crochet 2 or more stitches together, as indicated
sk	skip/skipped/skipping
sl st(s)	slip stitch(es)
sp(s)	space(s)/spaced
st(s)	stitch(es)
tog	together
tr	treble crochet
trtr	triple treble
WS	wrong side
yd(s)	yard(s)
yo	yarn over

YARN CONVERSION

OUNCES TO GRAMS		GRAMS TO OUNCES	
1	28.4	25	⅞
2	56.7	40	1⅔
3	85.0	50	1¾
4	113.4	100	3½

UNITED STATES		UNITED KINGDOM
sl st (slip stitch)	=	sc (single crochet)
sc (single crochet)	=	dc (double crochet)
hdc (half double crochet)	=	htr (half treble crochet)
dc (double crochet)	=	tr (treble crochet)
tr (treble crochet)	=	dtr (double treble crochet)
dtr (double treble crochet)	=	ttr (triple treble crochet)
skip	=	miss

Single crochet decrease (sc dec): (Insert hook, yo, draw lp through) in each of the sts indicated, yo, draw through all lps on hook.

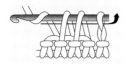

Example of 2-sc dec

Half double crochet decrease (hdc dec): (Yo, insert hook, yo, draw lp through) in each of the sts indicated, yo, draw through all lps on hook.

Example of 2-hdc dec

Reverse Single Crochet (reverse sc): Ch 1. Skip first st. [Working from left to right, insert hook in next st from front to back, draw up lp on hook, yo, and draw through both lps on hook.]

Chain (ch): Yo, pull through lp on hook.

Single crochet (sc): Insert hook in st, yo, pull through st, yo, pull through both lps on hook.

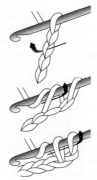

Double crochet (dc): Yo, insert hook in st, yo, pull through st, [yo, pull through 2 lps] twice.

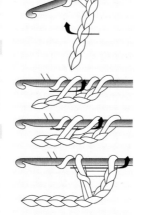

Double crochet decrease (dc dec): (Yo, insert hook, yo, draw lp through, yo, draw through 2 lps on hook) in each of the sts indicated, yo, draw through all lps on hook.

Example of 2-dc dec

Front loop (front lp) Back loop (back lp)

Front Loop   Back Loop

Front post stitch (fp): Back post stitch (bp): When working post st, insert hook from right to left around post st on previous row.

Back   Front

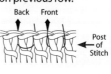

Post of Stitch

Half double crochet (hdc): Yo, insert hook in st, yo, pull through st, yo, pull through all 3 lps on hook.

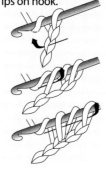

Double treble crochet (dtr): Yo 3 times, insert hook in st, yo, pull through st, [yo, pull through 2 lps] 4 times.

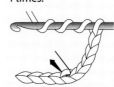

Treble crochet decrease (tr dec): Holding back last lp of each st, tr in each of the sts indicated, yo, pull through all lps on hook.

Example of 2-tr dec

Slip stitch (sl st): Insert hook in st, pull through both lps on hook.

Chain Color Change (ch color change) Yo with new color, draw through last lp on hook.

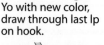

Double Crochet Color Change (dc color change) Drop first color, yo with new color, draw through last 2 lps of st.

Treble crochet (tr): Yo twice, insert hook in st, yo, pull through st, [yo, pull through 2 lps] 3 times.

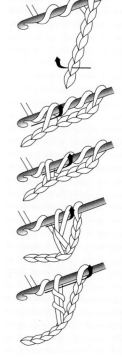

Metric Conversion Charts

METRIC CONVERSIONS

yards	x	.9144	=	metres (m)
yards	x	91.44	=	centimetres (cm)
inches	x	2.54	=	centimetres (cm)
inches	x	25.40	=	millimetres (mm)
inches	x	.0254	=	metres (m)

centimetres	x	.3937	=	inches
metres	x	1.0936	=	yards

INCHES INTO MILLIMETRES & CENTIMETRES (Rounded off slightly)

inches	mm	cm	inches	cm	inches	cm	inches	cm
1/8	3	0.3	5	12.5	21	53.5	38	96.5
1/4	6	0.6	5 1/2	14	22	56	39	99
3/8	10	1	6	15	23	58.5	40	101.5
1/2	13	1.3	7	18	24	61	41	104
5/8	15	1.5	8	20.5	25	63.5	42	106.5
3/4	20	2	9	23	26	66	43	109
7/8	22	2.2	10	25.5	27	68.5	44	112
1	25	2.5	11	28	28	71	45	114.5
1 1/4	32	3.2	12	30.5	29	73.5	46	117
1 1/2	38	3.8	13	33	30	76	47	119.5
1 3/4	45	4.5	14	35.5	31	79	48	122
2	50	5	15	38	32	81.5	49	124.5
2 1/2	65	6.5	16	40.5	33	84	50	127
3	75	7.5	17	43	34	86.5		
3 1/2	90	9	18	46	35	89		
4	100	10	19	48.5	36	91.5		
4 1/2	115	11.5	20	51	37	94		

KNITTING NEEDLES CONVERSION CHART

Canada/U.S.	0	1	2	3	4	5	6	7	8	9	10	10½	11	13	15
Metric (mm)	2	2¼	2¾	3¼	3½	3¾	4	4½	5	5½	6	6½	8	9	10

CROCHET HOOKS CONVERSION CHART

Canada/U.S.	1/B	2/C	3/D	4/E	5/F	6/G	8/H	9/I	10/J	10½/K	N
Metric (mm)	2.25	2.75	3.25	3.5	3.75	4.25	5	5.5	6	6.5	9.0

Irish Crochet is published by DRG, 306 East Parr Road, Berne, IN 46711. Printed in USA. Copyright © 2011 DRG.
All rights reserved. This publication may not be reproduced in part or in whole without written permission from the publisher.

RETAIL STORES: If you would like to carry this pattern book or any other DRG publications, visit DRGwholesale.com

Every effort has been made to ensure that the instructions in this publication are complete and accurate.
We cannot, however, take responsibility for human error, typographical mistakes or variations in individual work.
Please visit AnniesCustomerCare.com to check for pattern updates.

ISBN: 978-1-59635-369-5   1 2 3 4 5 6 7 8